Drunkard's Refuge

Drunkard's Refuge

The Lessons of the New York State
Inebriate Asylum

John W. Crowley

AND

William L. White

University of Massachusetts Press

Amherst and Boston

Copyright © 2004 by University of Massachusetts Press
Printed in the United States of America

LC 2003016299
ISBN 1-55849-430-8

Designed by Jack Harrison
Set in Berthold Walbaum Book by Graphic Composition, Inc.
Printed and bound by The Maple-Vail Book Manufacturing Group

Library of Congress Cataloging-in-Publication Data

Crowley, John William, 1945–
Drunkard's refuge : the lessons of the New York State Inebriate Asylum /
John W. Crowley and William L. White
p. cm.
Includes bibliographical references and index.
ISBN 1-55849-430-8 (cloth : alk. paper)
1. New York State Inebriate Asylum–History.
2. Alcoholism–Hospitals–New York (State)–Binghamton–History.
3. Alcoholism–Treatment–New York (State)–Binghamton–History.
4. Alcoholics–Rehabilitation–New York (State)–Binghamton–History.
5. Turner, J. Edward, 1822–1889. I. White, William L., 1947– II. Title.

RC564.74.N7 C76 2004
362.292′8′09747–dc22
2003016299

British Library Cataloguing in Publication data are available.

Contents

Preface

The authors have spent most of the past decade writing articles and books about the history of alcohol addiction, treatment, and recovery in America. Our earlier projects kept leading us back to the important yet mysterious story of the first medically directed addiction treatment facility, the New York State Inebriate Asylum, and the man who founded it, Dr. Joseph Edward Turner. Although parts of this story still remain hidden, owing to the absence of the personal papers of Turner and other key figures, we were able to discover archival materials that fill in crucial gaps about the founder and his institution. For the first time, a full chronology can be presented and its contemporary import explored.

We are telling this story for a particular audience: individuals working within or living within the worlds of addiction treatment and recovery. Our decision to focus on this audience was based on our belief that there was much here that had meaning to present-day treatment and recovery movements. This book, then, was not cast as a monograph aimed at temperance historians.

With a broader readership in mind, we also wanted to present our work in a particular way. After setting the background in chapter 1, we let the protagonists tell this story in their own words to the extent allowed by available resources. Chapters 2, 3, and 4 focus on Turner's vision of a national inebriate asylum, the battle for control over the New York State Inebriate Asylum, and the factors that led to Turner's banishment from the field and the asylum's collapse. It is our hope that readers will be thrust into the very heart of the story and come to identify with our long-deceased central characters. The final chapter explores quite directly what those voices from the past have to tell us about the present and future of addiction treatment.

This book arrives at a time when the modern field of addiction treatment is confronting threats to its essential character and future. Those threats involve challenges to the field's core ideas, clinical practices, and economic infrastructure. Many people who work within it or otherwise support its efforts have little awareness of a similar crisis more than a century ago that led to the collapse of America's first medical institution for the treatment of addiction and of the larger network of mutual aid societies and addiction treatment institutions. More important, they are unaware of the forces inside and outside the field that contributed, and could again contribute, to this demise. It is into that turbulent world of treatment and recovery in the nineteenth century that we invite the reader.

This is a story about a charismatic physician, his vision, and the fate of the historic institution that he created. It is a story of plots and intrigues, charges and countercharges, criminal accusations and indictments, and the plundering of an institution. It is a story that contains important insights into America's response to alcohol and other drug problems and even deeper insights into forces that can create and destroy service organizations.

As this book goes to press, a new recovery advocacy movement struggles to be born; if successful, it will again redefine how current culture views alcoholism and the alcoholic. We conclude by describing this movement and exploring what lessons from Dr. J. Edward Turner and the history of the New York State Inebriate Asylum might apply to this new movement.

Before closing this invitation to the reader to enter the world of alcoholism and its treatment in the nineteenth century, we want to acknowledge those individuals who first invited us into this world. Jim Baumohl and Robin Room paved the way with their pioneering research into the inebriate asylum era. Others who helped illuminate the early history of addiction and its treatment in America include David Musto, Harry Gene Levine, David Courtwright, Sarah Tracy, Leonard Blumberg, and Bill Pittman. We would be remiss if we did not thank Ernie Kurtz as well for his continued feedback and encouragement of our work. Finally, we are indebted to the Broome County Historical Society and the Illinois Addiction Studies Archives for access to their collections.

A Chronology of the New York State Inebriate Asylum

1822   Joseph Edward Turner is born in Bath, Maine, on 5 October.

1843   Turner abandons his medical practice to study new approaches to treatment of inebriety in Scotland, France, and England, performing postmortem dissections of more than 350 inebriates.

1845   Turner writes "circulars" to physicians, clergy, and judges soliciting their ideas about the treatment of inebriates.

1848–50   Turner travels to Russia, Germany, France, Italy, and England for further study of medical treatment of the inebriate.

1851   First state prohibition law is passed in Maine.

1852–53   Turner files application to New York legislature for incorporation of an inebriate asylum.

1854   The New York legislature grants charter to the "United States Inebriate Asylum" in April.

1855   Idea of an inebriate asylum draws criticism, particularly from clergy.

1857   Name in charter is changed to "New York State Inebriate Asylum."

1858   City of Binghamton, New York, gives 250 acres for the asylum; cornerstone is laid.

1859   In response to a petition with 10,000 signatures, the state sets aside one-tenth of excise tax on liquor to support the asylum.

1862   Legislative effort to repeal the asylum's charter fails.

1862   Turner marries Gertrude Middlebrook in October.

1863   Another attempt to repeal asylum charter is successfully rebuffed by Turner.

1863   Two fires at the asylum within two months cause substantial damage.

1864   First patients are admitted in June but only forty between February 1865 and February 1866.

1864   Fire guts unfinished north wing in September.

1865 Dr. Willard Parker becomes president of board; early conflict with Turner rapidly escalates.

1866 Dr. Turner is fired by board on June 25, reinstated in July, but forced out in September when the board shuts off all construction and supplies; board also files charges of arson, accusing Turner of having set the 1863 fires at the asylum—a charge for which he was indicted but never tried.

1867 Turner officially resigns his superintendent position and receives a settlement of $35,000 from the board.

1867 Asylum reopened under leadership of Dr. Albert Day.

1867 Turner moves to Wilton, Connecticut.

1868 Patients found the Ollapod Club, a literary and social support club within the asylum.

1870 There is a fire at the asylum that Dr. Day is accused of setting; Day resigns in May.

1870–73 Dr. Daniel G. Dodge heads the asylum.

1870 The American Association for the Cure of Inebriety is founded; Turner never joins because of his conflict with Parker, one of the founding members.

1873–75 Dr. Lyman Congdon heads the asylum.

1875–77 Dr. Dodge returns as head of the asylum.

1875 Turner tries to establish a hospital for female inebriates in Connecticut; plans are blocked by reports of earlier events in New York; charter for women's hospital is repealed in 1885.

1876 Turner's renewed attempt to regain control of the New York State Inebriate Asylum fails.

1878–79 Dr. Moreau Morris heads the asylum.

1879 Declared a failure by Governor Lucius Robinson, the asylum is sold by the board to the state of New York for $1.00.

1881 Facility reopened as an insane asylum.

1889 Dr. Turner dies 24 July in Wilton, Connecticut, at age sixty-six.

1909 The American Society for the Study of Alcohol and Other Narcotics (formerly the American Association for the Cure of Inebriety) places a marker on the grave of Dr. Joseph Edward Turner as a "token and instance of their love, gratitude and respect."

Drunkard's Refuge

1

"What Shall We Do with the Inebriate?"

Alcohol was ubiquitous in early colonial America. Its pervasiveness was a reflection of the European drinking practices brought to America and the lack of alternative beverages. In an era lacking effective water purification procedures and pasteurization, alcohol was thought to be essential to health and longevity. Community life centered on the tavern, and drinking alcohol was integral to virtually all social institutions and all social interactions. By law, taverns were located close to churches; political meetings and voting occurred at the tavern; workers were provided periodic alcoholic refreshment throughout the day; wages were partially paid in alcohol; alcohol was freely used in medicine; and the first colleges brought breweries to campus to supply alcohol for faculty and students. Yet although men, women, and children consumed alcohol every day and throughout the day, there is little evidence of widespread drunkenness—perhaps because of the social stigma attached to public drunkenness—until new patterns of alcohol consumption emerged in the aftermath of the Revolutionary War. These patterns included a more than threefold increase in per capita alcohol consumption between 1780 and 1830, the shift in preference from fermented alcohol (beer, wine, cider) to distilled liquor (particularly rum and whiskey), and new patterns of disruptive binge drinking by young men unattached to family or community.[1]

The increase in alcohol consumption during the late eighteenth and early nineteenth centuries was so dramatic in its personal and social effects that religious and political leaders became alarmed that drunkenness was threatening the very future of the new republic. The question

"What shall we do with the inebriate?" was repeatedly raised, passionately debated, and answered with a myriad of legal, religious, medical, and social remedies. In their collective impact, these measures eventually cut annual per capita alcohol consumption by two-thirds from the peak level of seven gallons reached in 1830. (For perspective, American annual per capita alcohol consumption in recent years has been below two gallons.)[2]

One historically unprecedented response to the alcohol crisis was the founding of institutions whose sole purpose was to transform the confirmed drunkard into a sober citizen. This chapter explores the rise and fall of such institutions and the new professional field on which Dr. Joseph Edward Turner and the New York State Inebriate Asylum exerted such a significant influence.

The Call for Reform

In the late eighteenth and early nineteenth centuries, Americans long accustomed to the pervasive presence of fermented and distilled beverages came to realize that people could become "addicted" to alcohol.[3] Four prominent leaders issued alarms about growing alcohol-related problems.

In 1774, Anthony Benezet published *The Mighty Destroyer Displayed*, the first American treatise on alcoholism. Benezet's background as a respected teacher, hospital manager, philanthropist, and social reformer added weight to his concern about drinking practices in colonial America. Alcohol had become a staple of colonial life because it was believed to possess powers to ward off the illness and death associated with contaminated water. Benezet challenged this view by extolling the virtues of water and attacking the myth of alcohol's health-enhancing properties. He rebutted the idea of alcohol as a gift from God by depicting it as a "bewitching poison" that was creating "dram-drinkers bound in slavery." In one of the earliest American allusions to the addictive properties of alcohol and the progressiveness of such addiction, Benezet noted the tendency of drunkards to lose their power of self-control over alcohol intake: "Drops beget drams, and drams beget more drams, till they become to be without weight or measure." He warned, moreover, that excessive drinking had moved beyond society's scoundrels to take possession of some of the brightest and most industrious of citizens. He argued that the plan of generating government income from the sale of alcohol was ill conceived and counterproductive, as no government could long sustain itself on revenues generated by a product that destroyed those who purchased it.[4]

Benezet's opening salvo was followed in 1784 by Dr. Benjamin Rush's *Inquiry into the Effects of Ardent Spirits on the Human Mind and Body.* Rush's status as Benezet's student, a signer of the Declaration of Independence, and the most prominent physician in the new republic generated wide readership for his pamphlet. The American temperance movement can rightly be said to have begun with the publication of his *Inquiry.*[5] Rush outlined the sources of intemperance (including heredity), catalogued the signs of chronic drunkenness, and declared this state an "odious disease" and a "disease induced by a vice." Presenting a medicalized view of drunkenness, Rush defined it as a condition that should be recognized and treated by the physician. He confirmed Benezet's observation about the addictiveness and progressiveness of intemperance and described several potential treatments for chronic drunkenness. In a follow-up essay in 1810, titled "Plan for an Asylum for Drunkards to be called the Sober House," Rush became the first American to call for the creation of special facilities to care for the chronic drunkard.[6]

In 1825, the Reverend Lyman Beecher delivered and then published his *Six Sermons on the Nature, Occasions, Signs, Evils, and Remedy of Intemperance.* Beecher's words formed a bridge between prevailing moral and emerging medical views of drunkenness. He declared that the intemperate were "addicted to the sin," that drinking was fueled by the drunkard's "insatiable desire to drink," and that bouts of intemperance accelerated progressively. Beecher was the first to describe the early warning signs that marked the loss of volitional control over alcohol consumption and concluded his final sermon by declaring, "Intemperance is a disease as well as a crime, and were any other disease as contagious, of as marked symptoms, and as mortal, to pervade the land, it would create universal consternation."[7]

In the 1830s one of America's most prominent physicians, Dr. Samuel Woodward, took up Rush's call for the creation of special asylums for the treatment of the inebriate. Woodward portrayed intemperance as a "physical disease which preys upon his [the drunkard's] health and spirits . . . making him a willing slave to his appetite" and declared that intemperance was too much a hereditary and physical disease to be ameliorated by solely moral means. He believed that this disorder could be medically treated and that its cure was contingent upon total abstinence from alcohol ("nothing stimulating, both now and forever").[8] Woodward helped spur calls by other influential physicians, such as Dr. Eli Todd, for more medically oriented approaches to the problem of inebriety.

One can see in the writings of Benezet, Rush, Beecher, and Woodward a cluster of ideas foundational to an emerging medical conception of addiction to alcohol: biological predisposition, drug toxicity, morbid appetite (craving), pharmacological tolerance, disease progression, inability to refrain from drinking, loss of volitional control over quantity, and a detailed accounting of the biological, psychological, and social consequences of chronic drunkenness. These writings also reflect the growing belief that the only reliable and permanent solution for this disease of drunkenness is complete abstinence from alcohol. Rush's view that "'Taste not, handle not, touch not' should be inscribed upon every vessel that contains spirits in the house of a man who wishes to be cured of habits of intemperance" was extended by Beecher, Woodward, and others to include abstinence from all intoxicating beverages, including the beer and wine that Rush had deemed innocuous, if not beneficial.

There is also in these writings a struggle to distinguish drunkenness as a vice from drunkenness caused by disease. They defined the "disease" of chronic intemperance not as intoxication but as an "ungovernable appetite" that overwhelms the choice and control of alcohol intake. What these early American writings on alcohol suggested was not so much that intemperance was a disease *instead* of a vice as that intemperance was a vice that could *become* a disease.[9]

Benezet, Rush, Beecher, and Woodward presented what to their contemporaries were controversial ideas that demanded a radical reconceptualization of the drunkard and drunkenness. In this new view, alcohol itself was reimagined. The "Good Creature of God" became the potentially poisonous "Demon Rum," and the chronic drunkard was understood less as a person who was bad and deserving of condemnation than one who was sick and deserving of help.[10] The new republic's religious, medical, political, and economic elite thrust on the citizenry a new view of alcohol, particularly of ardent spirits, a view that they believed would ensure the future health and progress of the country.

The redefinition of chronic drunkenness in terms of disease rather than moral depravity was based upon rapidly expanding knowledge about the physical effects of excessive alcohol consumption. This new knowledge, which ranged from the first studies of delirium tremens to the discovery of the toxic effects of alcohol on the stomach, blood, and nervous system, reached a pinnacle in 1849 in the work of the Swedish physician Magnus Huss. Huss's landmark study detailed the organ systems affected by chronic alcohol exposure and gave the resulting condition a new name. "These symptoms are formed in such a particular way that they form a disease group in themselves and thus merit being designated and described as a definite disease. . . . It is this group of symptoms which I wish to designate by the name *Alcoholismus chronicus.*"[11]

The works of Rush, Woodward, and Huss called attention to the newly christened condition of "alcoholism" as a problem that physicians should study and treat. As doctors took up this challenge, the terms "drunkenness" and "intemperance" gave way to a more medicalized language that designated both the newly defined disease and its sufferer: *inebriety/ inebriate, dipsomania/dipsomaniac, alcoholism/alcoholic.*

The emergence of a "disease concept" of alcoholism, upon which many later treatment efforts would be based, was not without its controversies. Clergy and physicians alike attacked the concept as providing an excuse for sin and irresponsibility. Even early advocates of the disease concept expressed ambivalence about this new way of viewing drunkenness. Dr. William Sweetser, in his medical dissertation on intemperance, reflects such ambivalence when he proclaims that intemperance is a disease produced by voluntary acts and then laments: "I feel convinced that should the opinion ever prevail that intemperance is a disease like fever, mania, etc., and no moral turpitude be affixed to it, drunkenness, if possible, will spread itself even to a more alarming extent than at present."[12]

In 1832 a Dr. Springwater, well known as a temperance advocate, expressed the way in which medical and moral views of alcoholism could coexist. After proclaiming intemperance to be a disease of the stomach whose only cure was in abandonment of the irritating agent, alcohol, he went on to describe the victim of this disease: "He [the drunkard] stalks about like a moral pestilence, scattering his vile contagion with every breath. He is a walking plague, a living death. He caters for hell. He recruits for the devil. Oh! What a deadly damp he breathes on his country, creating a poisonous influence, and scattering a moral and physical pestilence upon its shores!"[13]

Criticism of the disease concept intensified throughout the nineteenth century. The Reverend J. E. Todd in his 1882 treatise, *Drunkenness a Vice, Not a Disease*, argued (1) that drunkards were not diseased but morally inferior, (2) that efforts to "treat" drunkards were doomed to failure because they rarely ever reformed, and (3) that the stigma upon drunkenness should be more deeply impressed rather than erased. Todd declared: "I must protest vigorously all this cloaking of the vice of drunkenness, . . . this calling drunkards 'diseased men.' . . . Let us call things by their right names. The sooner that the drunkard takes the place in the estimation to which he belongs, the sooner will young men hesitate about applying for the situation. . . . Why should the drunkard not enter the kingdom of God? Because he is wicked; one of the most wicked men alive. That is all."[14]

The animosity that the disease concept of alcohol addiction could arouse is further typified in the remarks of Dr. C. W. Earle of Chicago in 1880: "It is becoming altogether too customary in these days to speak of vice as disease. . . . That the responsibility of taking the opium or whiskey . . . is to be excused and called a disease, I am not willing for one moment to admit, and I propose to fight this pernicious doctrine as long as is necessary."[15] Criticism of the disease concept did not dampen the movement for medical experiments in the treatment of inebriety, but these experiments unfolded within an adversarial context that greatly influenced their development and eventual fate.

Two Temperance Movements

Addiction treatment institutions in the nineteenth century existed within a unique cultural moment. Immigration and dramatic population growth contributed to a rising concern about a plethora of social and public health problems and about civil disorder, of which public drunkenness was the most visible symbol. A reform spirit sought to address social problems through the development and refinement of such institutions as almshouses, orphanages, hospitals, prisons, and insane asylums.[16] The struggle to professionalize medical practice and the explosive growth of a proprietary drug industry also shaped the evolution of addiction treatments. Yet all these significant contextual influences pale in comparison with the influence of the American temperance movement that Benjamin Rush and his colleagues had set in motion.

The voices of Benezet, Rush, Beecher, and Woodward stirred a social debate that polarized America for more than a century into "Wet" and "Dry" camps. As the temperance movement gained momentum, it absorbed such cultural forces as feminism, racism, and anti-Catholicism, thus expanding beyond its original stated purpose. Nevertheless, it was a direct consequence of a dramatic increase in alcohol consumption and alcohol-related problems, and its primary goal remained the resolution and prevention of such problems.

Early on, there were two strains within this movement. The mainstream "gospel temperance" at first sought to attack America's alcohol problems by promoting moderate drinking practices and, in particular, by eliminating the use of distilled spirits. Between 1825 and 1850, however, the campaign shifted toward promotion of complete abstinence from all intoxicating beverages. The methods of gospel temperance included education, inducements to sign a lifetime pledge of abstinence (teetotalism), and advocacy of a legal ban on the sale of alcohol. Individual drunkards sought haven within the movement, but rescuing the drunkard was never its major purpose. Instead, the objective of gospel temperance was to let the existing generation of drunkards die off while preventing the creation of new drunkards to take their place.

The mainstream temperance organizations that developed between 1830 and 1860 saw alcohol as a poison to which everyone was vulnerable. In this view, the so-called moderate drinker was simply a precursor to the drunkard, who was, in turn, viewed as "loathsome and an abomination." The answer to the problems created by drink was to call for the overthrow of King Alcohol, just as the colonies had overthrown their equally tyrannous King George. From the creation of the first American temperance organizations through the passage of the Eighteenth Amendment to the Constitution in 1919, the focus of the mainstream temperance movement was not on the alcoholic but on alcohol and the institution of the saloon, which had become associated with vice, crime, disease, and political corruption. Temperance advocates exhibited considerable pessimism about reforming the drunkard; their aim was to prevent people from initiating alcohol consumption and to coax the occasional tippler to make a lifetime pledge of abstinence before his or her inevitable slide into drunkenness.

Within gospel temperance, however, there emerged a more specialized movement whose exclusive goal *was* the reclamation of the drunkard
through "rescue work." "Therapeutic temperance" not only generated
many alcoholic mutual aid societies but also fostered the organization
and support of homes for the care of inebriates. It should be noted, however, that this new definition of the inebriate as someone worthy of rescue
had its limitations. First, the medical model of inebriety was extended primarily to men, not to women, whose excessive alcohol consumption continued throughout the nineteenth century to be defined almost exclusively
in moral terms. There were also class distinctions. The set of those worthy to be rescued was restricted primarily to men of means who, after
achieving some degree of success in life, had fallen on hard times as a
direct consequence of alcoholism. Those of less wealth and less noble histories were more likely to be viewed not as inebriates worthy of rescue
but as "common sots."

The focus on the worthy inebriate helped to create a cultural climate
within which more explicitly medicalized approaches to treatment flourished and institutions arose to bring help and hope to the inebriate.[17] Efforts to rescue and reform or rehabilitate the drunkard drew their inspiration from a most unlikely source.

The Washingtonian Movement

Although the history of sobriety-based mutual aid societies is often
thought to have begun with the 1935 founding of Alcoholics Anonymous,
there were in fact many such societies in eighteenth- and nineteenth-
century America. These ranged from Native American recovery "circles,"
dating from the 1730s to 1750s, to the recovery-focused fraternal temperance societies and ribbon reform clubs, named for the practice of their
members of wearing red, blue, or purple ribbons on their clothing, that
flourished between the mid-1840s and the 1870s.[18] Mutual aid societies relied on the power of the signed abstinence pledge, moral and religious reformation, sober fellowship, and service to other alcoholics to bolster the
newfound sobriety of their members.

The most prominent of such societies in total membership, geographi-
cal dispersion, cultural visibility, and enduring influence was the Washington Temperance Society. During the 1820s and 1830s, male alcoholics

had attempted to support their fragile sobriety through participation in local temperance societies but were rarely fully accepted by such groups, which were themselves in decline by the late 1830s. It was in this context that William Mitchell, David Anderson, Archibald Campbell, John Hoss, George Stears, and James McCurley, members of a drinking club at the Chase Tavern in Baltimore, Maryland, decided in April 1840 to start their own temperance society—an organization that was in its original conception to be a sober sanctuary for "sots" and "hard cases," contemporary terms for heavy drinkers. The growth of the Washingtonian movement was explosive (membership reached more than 500,000 within three years of its founding) and its effect on the larger culture in the early 1840s almost electric.[19] Its growth and visibility were due in great part to such men as John Gough and John Hawkins, who, after finding their own sobriety, joined the elite ranks of the nation's most charismatic temperance speakers. In the years between their recoveries and their deaths, the two men traveled some 650,000 miles to deliver more than 13,000 speeches. These temperance missionaries—or "reformed reformers," as they were often called—spent their lives carrying a message of hope for sobriety and personal redemption all over North America and Europe.[20]

The Washingtonian societies kept their members sober through such mechanisms as (1) public confession (storytelling) and commitment (pledge signing), (2) outreach to other alcoholics, (3) material assistance, and (4) sober recreation. The centerpiece of their program was the large "experience sharing" meeting, which marked a dramatic change in temperance movement activity. Rather than offering the moral entreaties of preachers or the dire warnings of physicians, the Washingtonian meetings enticed those present into telling their own stories of drunken debauchery and challenged inebriates to reclaim their sobriety and their manhood. The emotional power of such public displays briefly galvanized a culture unaccustomed to such displays of emotional intimacy. The Washingtonian meetings might be said to be one of America's first popular cultural phenomena. The movement also spawned Martha Washington Societies, which drew large numbers of women into rescue work with drunkards and fostered the first rescue work with female inebriates.

The demise of most Washingtonian societies was as rapid as their rise. By 1845, much of the energy of the movement had dissipated, and many local chapters restructured themselves as more formal and exclusive fraternal temperance societies. The downfall of the Washingtonians has been attributed to the loss of their closed meeting ("sots only") structure, dissension over outside political issues (particularly the question of the legal prohibition of alcohol), philosophical conflict with local religious groups, the lack of an enduring program of personal recovery, and their inability to sustain local leadership.

What the Washingtonian movement did do was to reinvigorate the larger temperance movement of which it was a part, spark continued mutual aid experiments, and inspire the lay and professional leadership who were about to champion and then build the world's first addiction treatment institutions.

The Rise of Addiction Treatment in America

Many social institutions were sharing responsibility for the care of nineteenth-century inebriates: jails, county farms, almshouses, sanatoria, water cure spas, and insane asylums.[21] It was their failure to control or rehabilitate inebriates that led to the development of a specialized, multibranched field of addiction treatment. There was also a growing belief that some drunkards needed more focused assistance than could be offered by such groups as the Washingtonians—although leaders of the early mutual aid societies did play crucial roles in the establishment of such institutions as the Washingtonian Homes in Boston (1857) and Chicago (1863). The newly founded inebriate "homes" viewed recovery as a process of moral reformation that relied on short voluntary stays and nonphysical methods of treatment. To the extent that inebriety was viewed as a disease in these homes, it was deemed a disease of the will, best treated in environments and by methods that would rehabilitate the inebriate's power of self-control. The rehabilitative emphasis lay on the establishment of a structured daily life, personal discipline, hard work, moral and religious education, and mutual support.

Medically focused treatment developed within the individual care provided by private physicians. "Alcoholism treatment" can be said to have begun when physicians shifted from ameliorating the medical consequences of alcoholism to seeking ways to alter what they perceived to be the essence of alcohol addiction: morbid craving and the loss of consistent control over alcohol intake. A few doctors began to specialize in addiction medicine and to advocate the creation of medically oriented inebriate asylums. These institutions, which grew directly from the efforts of reform-minded physicians, constitute a legacy built upon the earlier work of Rush and Woodward.

Inebriate *asylums,* in contrast to the inebriate *homes,* were directed by physicians, emphasized physical causes of inebriety, and utilized physical methods of treatment: drug therapies, aversion therapy, hydrotherapy, and electrical stimulation. Whereas the inebriate home emphasized brief, voluntary stays, the inebriate asylum emphasized legal restraint (commitment) for periods ranging from one year to "until the patient is cured."

The roots of a third, religiously oriented branch of the therapeutic temperance movement may be traced to the 1872 opening of the Water Street Mission in New York City. There, Jerry McAuley and his wife Maria, both redeemed alcoholics, inaugurated an urban mission movement that brought safe shelter and a message of hope to the destitute alcoholic. The weekly newspaper advertisement for the Water Street Mission said it all: "Everyone welcome, especially drunkards." McAuley and other alcoholic missionaries also played leadership roles in starting religiously oriented inebriate homes, notably the New York Christian Home for Intemperate Men. McAuley's missions were the forerunners of the Salvation Army and other urban mission programs that would come to serve the special needs of the Skid Row alcoholic. The missions and religion-based treatment institutions viewed recovery from addiction as a conversion process: first of religious awakening and then of living within a faith community that daily reaffirmed one's rebirth.[22]

On the business side, the nineteenth-century treatment industry ofered two varieties of treatment. First, there were private for-profit sanatoria and addiction cure institutes. Many of the latter—the Keeley Institutes, the Gatlin Institutes, the Neal Institutes, and the Oppenheimer Institutes—were franchised across the United States and made their founders quite wealthy. Less heralded local institutes and private sanatoria did not specialize in the treatment of inebriety but offered the advantage of discreet detoxification and convalescence for affluent alcoholics and addicts under such euphemistic diagnoses as nervous exhaustion or neurasthenia.

The second variety of proprietary treatment consisted of bottled home cures. Ironically, a patent medicine industry that aggressively promoted alcohol-, opium-, and cocaine-laced products—responsible for the accidental addiction of many Americans–began also to offer its own bottled addiction cures during the second half of the nineteenth century. Hangover and alcoholism remedies included the Hay-Litchfield Antidote and Knights Tonic for Inebriates. The White Star Secret Liquor Cure and the Boston Drug Cure for Drunkenness were promoted with the promise that wives could secretly treat their husbands' inebriety by surreptitiously pouring the potion into the men's food or drink. It seemed for a while as if everyone was getting into the addiction cure business. Even Sears, Roebuck & Company offered a fifty-cent cure for the liquor habit in its late nineteenth-century mail order catalogues.[23]

The expanding range of services for alcohol addicts embraced hundreds of individual practitioners, institutions, and businesses. Some of the early institutional providers of treatment joined together in 1870 to found the American Association for the Cure of Inebriety. The founding principles of the AACI posited that inebriety was a disease, that the disease could be either inherited or acquired, that the disease was treatable, and that the state bore a responsibility to provide such treatment. Two goals of the AACI were to build a new field of professional endeavor and to foster the professional legitimacy and credibility of that field. To that end, it became increasingly medicalized. Excluding proprietary cure institutes and bottled cure purveyors and openly attacking them as charlatans, AACI members called for state regulation of the burgeoning addiction treatment industry.[24]

The controversial centerpiece of the AACI, the disease concept of inebriety, was a source of external criticism–particularly from religious and temperance leaders–and a subject of periodic debate within the association itself.[25] Dr. Robert Harris, the head of the Franklin Reformatory for Inebriates in Philadelphia, attacked the disease theory as "a pernicious and dangerous fallacy," "a weak apology for the sin of drunkenness," and a "blasphemy against God." Harris charged that the disease theory was "destructive to the idea of free will" and that it relieved men of moral obligation and responsibility.[26] Many inebriety specialists tried to reconcile the idea of free will with the emerging concept of addiction and addictive disease–concepts that called into question the limits of human will. These discussions and debates about the causes, nature, and most effective treatment of alcoholism filled the pages of the AACI's *Journal of Inebriety* during the late nineteenth century.

A Man and an Institution

As the rise of alcohol and other drug consumption during the early nineteenth century led to a medicalized conception of addiction problems, one man's remarkable life and his controversial institution formed the bridge between the ideas of Benezet, Rush, and Woodward and the rise of institutions and a profession that specialized in the treatment of the inebriate. If there is any single person responsible for the birth of medically directed addiction treatment institutions in the United States, it is Dr. Joseph Edward Turner. If there is one institution that best captures the triumphs *and* tragedies of nineteenth-century addiction treatment, it is the very first and most beleaguered of such institutions: the New York State Inebriate Asylum. What follows is the story of the man, his institution, and what each has to teach us today about alcoholism treatment and recovery.

2

The Visionary J. Edward Turner

The founder of the New York State Inebriate Asylum at Binghamton chronicled that institution's history in exhaustive detail, but he kept his personal life to himself.[1] The biographical record is thin, especially concerning his formative years. These are the bare facts.[2]

Joseph Edward Turner was born in Bath, Maine (up the coast from Portland), on 5 October 1822. Through his father, Oakman, Turner could trace his American ancestry to 1641. Native to Ipswich, Massachusetts, Oakman Turner migrated to Woolwich, Maine, in 1807 and then to Bath in 1816 as one of that town's original settlers. Two years later he married Mary Hodgkins, whose parents had emigrated from England to Ipswich in 1880. Mary Turner bore two children, Joseph and Mary. The son, who worked beside his father on the family farm and also at the Bath shipyards, attended the village academy and rose to the top of his class. After preparing at home for college, he decided instead to take medical training from a neighbor, a Dr. Hale.

American medicine was still in its horse-and-buggy days, more a trade than the profession it would become after the Civil War. As rural doctor's apprentice, Turner would have been expected to serve locally, but he ambitiously went on to attend two courses of medical lectures in Philadelphia. Duly licensed by the Maine Medical Society, he opened a practice in Trenton, New Jersey, about 1841.

Later, during Turner's troubles in Binghamton, his medical credentials were impugned, and he was dismissed as a bumpkin quack. It is fairer to

"The Founder," Dr. J. Edward Turner. From Turner,
History of the First Inebriate Asylum.

say that Turner was inexperienced as a physician and that he made few
strictly scientific contributions to the medical field. He was driven by
ambition and a particular dream.[3] When his career had scarcely begun,
Turner "became possessed," as his disciple T. D. Crothers puts it, "with
the idea of founding an inebriate asylum and gave up his work for that
purpose" (*MA*, 2). What can account for Turner's commitment to such a
cause—one that "wherever mentioned, at first was treated with derision
and contempt"? Resistance resulted only in redoubling Turner's dedication to the idea, "creating a more emphatic conviction of its truthful-
ness" (*S*, 302).

It is important to recognize, for one thing, that Turner's childhood environment was steeped in alcohol and its often dire effects. Maine (a part
of Massachusetts until 1820) was reputedly "the hardest-drinking state

in the Union" during the period when American alcohol consumption reached its historic peak. Down-Easters, according to one statistician, "spent on drink, every twenty years, a sum equivalent to the value of all the property in Maine."[4]

Neal Dow's Maine

Such sensational claims were corroborated by Neal Dow, the state's "Napoleon" of prohibition. "At the time of the admission of Maine to the Union, and for thirty years thereafter," Dow stated in his 1898 autobiography, "her people probably consumed more intoxicating liquor in proportion to their numbers than the people of any other state." Dow reported, for instance, that when the population of Portland numbered less than 4,000, there were more than eighty-one licensed liquor dealers. By 1823, the year after Turner's birth, when Portland's population reached 9,000, the manufacture and sale of spirits were more than keeping pace, with two hundred licensed dealers plus innumerable unlicensed dram shops, as well as seven distilleries and two breweries. It was customary for laborers to knock off for drinking breaks at eleven and four; the city bell obligingly rang the hours.[5]

Heavy drinking was by no means confined to Maine's cities. "Every village had its rum shops, and those of any pretensions, scores of them," observed D. R. Locke, in an investigation for the *Toledo (Ohio) Blade.* "Lawlessness and order-breaking were common; brawls and fighting were invariable on election days and all public occasions, and, in short, the state was demoralized as a state wholly given over to rum always is." The farms, Locke continues, were even worse than the towns. "You might ride for miles without seeing a painted house, a sound fence, or windows without broken glass in them. . . . Crops were meager and uncertain, for the rum mills confiscated the time necessary to the proper working of the farm."[6]

Dow attributed such rampant drunkenness to peculiar historical circumstances. Maine had supplied a disproportionate share of troops both to the Revolutionary War and to the War of 1812. Hence, large numbers of Maine's young men acquired intemperate habits under harsh wartime conditions, habits that persisted into adult lives rendered equally harsh by economic adversity. Given that the largest industries—fishing, shipping, and lumbering–called men to rough work away from women and thus apart from the refining influence of domesticity, there was all the more cause for inebriety to flourish. Maine, furthermore, was party to the Caribbean trade in which lumber was exchanged for West Indian rum and molasses, which was locally distilled into even more rum. The supply of cheap liquor was virtually unlimited to a population that was among the poorest in the nation.

If Maine was notorious for drunkenness, however, it also became synonymous with prohibition through the passage in 1851 of the Maine Law, of which Dow was the political mastermind. Temperance reform had come early to the state, under the leadership of its clergy. In 1812, only four years after the first local American temperance society sprang up near Saratoga, New York, similar groups were founded in Portland, Saco, and Bath (Turner's hometown), and they proliferated during the 1820s.[7] The State Temperance Society of Maine was organized in 1832, the year before General James Appleton, the intrepid "Father of Prohibition," moved to Portland from Massachusetts, where he had helped to draft the first American dry law. Appleton radicalized Maine's temperance movement, plunging into Portland politics and sponsoring an anti-drink measure (which failed by a single vote). Dow modeled his own reform career on Appleton's activism, taking it to new extremes of combativeness.

Dow and Turner

It may be useful to think of Dow in counterpoint to Turner, whose campaign for an inebriate asylum was comparably fanatical. Legendarily hotheaded, Dow regarded temperance as a holy war in which his own role was divinely ordained. His ironclad self-certainty blunted every challenge to his own convictions, and his stamina knew no bounds. During the 1840s, for example, he canvassed the entire state of Maine, "lecturing, buttonholing politicians, and helping establish local restrictions on liquor sales. In 1846 alone, he logged some four thousand miles and gathered over forty thousand signatures on a petition for state prohibition."[8]

Turner lacked Dow's belligerence, but he clung to his own ideas with the same invincible tenacity and crusaded for his cause with charismatic intensity. Crother remarks of Turner:

> There was a certain self confidence and poise in his manner and calm re-
> serve that was not disturbed by outer conditions and gave the impression of
> a man of power and force.
>
> His manner was dignified, sympathetic and intense. In the presentation
> of the great purposes of his life he was simply overwhelming, not only in
> suggestion, but a flood of arguments, facts and illustrations which were
> convincing.
>
> There was a certain magnetism about the way in which he presented the
> facts which grew with every experience and very few persons could listen
> to him without being impressed with their reality. (*MA*, 3)

Turner also shared with Dow a compassionate perspective on inebriates, if not those who exploited them. In a passage about his childhood
awakening to the problem of intemperance, Dow voiced sentiments with
which Turner identified:

> I saw health impaired, capacity undermined, employment lost. I saw wives
> and children suffering from the drinking habits of husbands and fathers
> long before the latter could be said to have become drunkards, in the parl-
> ance of the day. I saw that, as a rule, neither industry, thrift, prudence, sav-
> ing nor comfort was to be found where indulgence in intoxicants prevailed.
> Called often to render assistance in these cases, my indignation at the men
> who brought so much suffering upon their families for the gratification, as
> it then seemed to me, of a mere taste for liquor, softened into pity and sym-
> pathy when I found them the apparently helpless victims of a controlling
> appetite that was dragging them to ruin. My observation of this had its effect
> in determining the position I afterwards took.[9]

For Dow, indignation prevailed; the position he took pitted him against
the drunkard-makers. He never concerned himself, as Norman H. Clark
says, with "why men drink." There is "no psychological or philosophical
reflection of any significance in his rich reminiscences. He worried only
about what drinking did to drunkards, and this was no abstraction; he
saw inefficiency, irresponsibility, violence."[10] For Turner, by contrast, pity
prevailed; the position he took allied him with drunkards themselves. He
never concerned himself with the politics of reform.[11] But in regarding
inebriates as "helpless victims of a controlling appetite"–indeed, of a disease–Turner, like Dow, minimized the drunkard's capacity to help himself or to be helped by other than authoritarian intervention. For both
men, controlling alcohol, either the supply of or demand for it, was the
vital issue.

Turner's Vision

Whether or not Turner was much aware of Dow is unknown, as is the extent of Turner's cognizance of the temperance tempest that surrounded his upbringing—though he could not have remained untouched by it. He also had personal reasons for his interest in inebriates. Like Dow, he had met the Demon Rum face to face: at the age of eighteen he nursed an uncle through periodic binges that often climaxed in delirium tremens. Turner later affirmed the belief he acquired at that time, "that inebriety was a disease and must be treated in hospitals the same as other diseases." He cited one other formative incident: a close friend got drunk and assaulted him, only to recover within a few hours but recall nothing of the violent episode (*MA*, 5). When another friend (or perhaps this same one) later died from drinking, Turner felt frustrated that he had been unable to save him, lacking the "power of restraint to be found only in an asylum."[12]

Turner's curiosity may have been aroused during his medical study by the small body of scientific literature that conceptualized inebriety as a disease. Crothers mentions Benjamin Rush's famous pamphlet as well as specific papers by Dr. Eli Todd of the Hartford Insane Asylum and Dr. Samuel Woodward of Worcester. But Turner may just as likely have read Thomas Trotter or other English authorities.[13] In any event, as Crothers recognizes, what galvanized Turner's dedication to the cause of inebriates was the eruption of the Washingtonian revival—contemporaneous with his first years in medical practice—which accelerated "recognition of the physical nature of the disorder" and also seemed to prophesy "the coming of inebriate asylums and hospitals where they could be housed and cured" (*MA*, 6).

One way of understanding Turner's later crisis at the New York State Inebriate Asylum is to see him as coming into conflict with the Washingtonian approach to treatment, espoused by his antagonists. If so, then Turner's impressions of the Washingtonians during the 1840s would be especially revealing. Unfortunately, this is one of many blanks in the record. All we know is that Turner abandoned his medical practice in 1843, at the height of the Washingtonian excitation, and traveled abroad to consult with European experts even as he promoted his own plans for an inebriate asylum.

His ideas fit into what David J. Rothman has called "the discovery of the asylum": a revolution in social practice after 1820 that led to the sudden and simultaneous erection of "penitentiaries for the criminal, asylums for the insane, almshouses for the poor, orphan asylums for homeless children, and reformatories for delinquents." The origins of this development lay in Enlightenment Europe's movement in the same direction of providing more specialized and humane treatment for deviant groups. But American institutions also expressed a native concern, during the turbulent Jacksonian period, with both the perils and the possibilities of social instability: "Legislators, philanthropists, and local officials, as well as students of poverty, crime, and insanity were convinced that the nation faced unprecedented dangers and unprecedented opportunities. The asylum, they believed, could restore a necessary social balance to the new republic, and at the same time eliminate long-standing problems. At once nervous and enthusiastic, distressed and optimistic, they set about constructing and arranging the institutions."[14]

In this light, Turner might be dubbed the Dorothea Dix of drunkards, attempting to extend her enlightened attitudes about insanity to inebriety as a previously unrecognized species of insanity—another disease entity in an expanding array of somatic psychiatric disorders, all of which were thought to be marked by discrete organic pathology (mainly brain lesions) and thus properly to be treated by nonpunitive medical methods. The notion of inebriety as a disease was not original with Turner; it had been evolving since the 1790s as part of the medicalization of insanity. But he embraced it with extraordinary fervor, and—this was the original stroke—he linked it to the contemporary asylum movement.

The true inspiration of Turner's cause, then, consisted not in his wishing to build an asylum but in his wishing to build one for *inebriates*. Thus the controversy he aroused centered not on the idea of an asylum per se—that was already unexceptionable among progressive thinkers—but on the moral and scientific legitimacy of applying the disease model to drunkards, who, if treated at all, had earlier been undistinguished from the poor, the criminal, and the demented and had, willy-nilly, been immured with them in almshouses, prisons, and insane asylums. In fact, as Rothman points out, the asylum movement had already begun to decline when Turner started his career, and the utopian ideal of "moral treatment" had devolved into expedient custodial incarceration by the time his asylum was receiving its first patients during the Civil War. The belatedness of Turner's mission may have been one factor in his struggle to realize it.

The Preparation and Planning Years

During his first European tour in the 1840s, Turner's aim was to school himself in the most advanced medical theories about the causes and treatment of inebriety. Learning little from the medical men of Glasgow and Edinburgh, whose own imbibing was notorious, he moved on to London and Paris. For two years he visited most of the major hospitals and asylums, collecting statistics and gathering physical evidence from the nearly 350 dissections and 460 postmortem examinations he performed on the cadavers of inebriates. Upon his return to America in 1845, he wrote up his findings in a series of circular letters "addressed to physicians, clergymen, judges, and coroners soliciting facts in their experience upon the physical, mental, moral, social, criminal, and economic status of the inebriate" (*S*, 303).

To the more than 3,000 circulars Turner sent out to doctors during the first three years of his inquiry, he received only 134 replies. The return rate was scarcely better among the other groups except (for no apparent reason) the seventy-four coroners, sixty-four of whom answered (*H*, 16). But Turner persevered, and he gained some attention as he made the rounds of hospitals in New York and Philadelphia, where he impressed such leading physicians as Valentine Mott and John W. Francis, both of whom became friends and loyal advocates for the inebriate asylum.

Turner returned to Europe in 1848, bound for Russia, where he frequented the hospitals and police courts of Moscow and St. Petersburg. On the same trip he carried his campaign to Germany, Italy, and again to France; he revisited England in 1850.[15] Turner seems to have thought, according to Crothers, "that he could get a personal endorsement and full recognition of his theory in the leading capitals of Europe, and with this he could command patronage and attention in this country" (*S*, 304). If so, the strategy failed resounding; although Turner was buoyed by the private sympathy, if not the public support, of foreign physicians, he was undoubtedly considered a crank by some of those with whom he sought to ingratiate himself. But he was impervious to discouragement. After six years of effort, says Crothers, "the little he had accomplished and stern opposition he had encountered would have, to most men, been evidence of the impossibility of the work. But to him it only roused a greater enthusiasm and energy and positive conviction in ultimate success" (*S,* 305).

Now we come to the phase of Turner's life that is more fully documented: the years of his single-minded and single-handed appeal to every prominent professional man with whom he could wheedle an interview–in sixteen years he claimed to have made "over seventy-thousand calls" (*H,* 19)[16]–for purposes of creating a stock company to build an inebriate asylum. The stock, fixed at $10 a share, was sold on the condition that $50,000 would be raised and that a charter would be obtained from a state legislature receptive to the project. Of the 3,000 persons first approached by Turner during four years of exhausting travel, much of it by night train, only sixty-six were willing to buy in, some of them under such strictures as that they would pay their subscriptions only when the asylum was actually built or when it produced its first cure. Turner pushed ahead. In 1852 he brought a charter application before the New York State Legislature. The proposal was assigned to committee during the next year's regular and extra sessions, and the political jockeying began. All the while Turner lobbied furiously, not only buttonholing the legislators themselves but also plying their constituents and campaigning against his most vocal critics. Friends with leverage were enlisted in the cause in the hope of neutralizing "the most stubborn opposition from clergy, medical men, and others, who" wrote Crother, "pronounced the whole scheme a fraud and disgrace to the intelligence of the country" (*S,* 306).

A bill was finally forced out of committee, and a charter was granted on 15 April 1854 to a corporation named, with legalistic redundancy, the United States Inebriate Asylum for the Reformation of the Poor and Destitute Inebriate.[17] Twenty interested parties, of 140 who had expressed sympathy, were ultimately willing to serve on the board of directors, but five meetings had to be called before a quorum could be secured. Despite a torrential rainstorm, an organizational meeting was held on 15 May 1854 in the Tract Society Building on Nassau Street in New York City. A dozen men adopted the articles of incorporation and elected officers: John D. Wright as president, N. A. Prince as registrar, and Turner himself as treasurer.

The treasurer was authorized to open the books and to receive subscriptions to the capital stock, two-thirds of which Turner alone had already sold or would sell before 1857. In fact, no other member of the board, all of whom had themselves subscribed, could raise a single dollar from his friends–for lack, one of them suggested, of Turner's silver-tongued persuasiveness. The board members believed that if the asylum were ever to be built, "the projector was the only man who could accomplish it" (*H*, 80). (An interim plan, never carried out, was to lease a building in New York and admit some patients immediately.) The need for more private subscriptions prompted the board to sponsor an informational public meeting at the Broadway Tabernacle on 7 November 1855. The event was widely advertised, and ministers were asked to announce it from their pulpits. But a few declined to cooperate, and "some of the religious and temperance papers offered serious opposition" (*S*, 307). Attendance was soberingly small; only eighty-two souls showed up to hear the addresses of two eminent clergymen, Henry W. Bellows and Roswell D. Hitchcock.

The board also issued an appeal for investment through a pamphlet that clarified objectives and implicitly answered objections. It stressed the proposed asylum's economic advantages to the community: separating inebriates from criminals and paupers and thereby reducing the costs of prisons and almshouses; operating on a self-sustaining basis, with patients involved in the care and improvement of the facility; restoring inebriates to gainful employment outside. "This institution," the public (including skeptical clergy) was assured, "is not designed to conflict with any other method for recovering the inebriate. There is no asylum similar to it in this or any other country" (quoted in *H*, 58).

As fund-raising languished, it became obvious to Turner that the asylum would never succeed without direct funding by the state. So during the legislative session of 1857, he and his allies appeared before the Financial Committee of the New York State Assembly, "pleading for ten per cent of the excise moneys of the counties as a gift to the Asylum for the medical treatment of the 'poor and destitute inebriate.'" Turner was, in effect, asking New York to tithe its profits from the sale of liquor on the reasonable grounds that "if the State permits a revenue to arise from this traffic, it should amply provide for the disease it creates, by building and founding the most complete hospitals in the world, cost what they may." With a rhetorical flourish, Turner added, "Has not the State a greater interest in the medical treatment of the drunkard which will rescue him from a premature grave than in the completion of her canals?" (*H*, 44–46).

Site Selection and Construction

At first, one and only one lawmaker was convinced. The legislature did change the corporation's name to the New York State Inebriate Asylum, and in anticipation of victory Turner opened a search for an appropriate site. He made the selection process into a contest of municipal pride: whichever community provided the finest location would win.

A gift of 250 choice acres was accepted in May 1858 from the city of Binghamton. The site conformed to the pastoral ideal of the nineteenth-century asylum, the typically rural setting of which was calculated to foster mental recreation as well as physical recuperation.[18] As the poet Alfred B. Street magniloquently effused during the 1858 dedication ceremony:

> Here—where the landscape spreads its charms abroad,
> peerless picture from the hand of God,
> Hill, meadow, vale, to cultivation won,
> And, in the midst, bright, leaf-bowered Binghamton;
> Where Susquehanna, radiant with its smiles,
> Crowned with his emerald diadem of isles,
> King of the realm! caressing and caressed,
> Clasps his sweet bride, Chenango, to his breast;
> A scene, whose soft and soothing sense shall find
> Way to the struggling, renovating mind. (*H*, 139)

Perched on a hillock two miles east of the city,[19] the location indeed afforded an idyllic view of the Susquehanna and Chenango Valleys as well as the confluence of the rivers themselves. Since there was abundant land for agriculture, especially after the asylum's property was augmented by 150 acres, some patients later helped to run a farm as occupational therapy.

The push behind Binghamton's successful bid came, as a local historian has established, from five powerful citizens: "Elias Hawley; Sherman D. Phelps, banker, businessman and future mayor of Binghamton; Oliver C. Crocker, a Broome County Assemblyman in 1847; Major Augustus Morgan, founder of the 'Weekly Broome Republican,' stagecoach line owner and co-owner of the Binghamton Coffee House; and Samuel H. P. Hall, a prominent Court Street businessman." Their motives are obscure, but Karla M. Eisch points out that intemperance had become increasingly problematic in the city since the completion of the Chenango Canal in 1836, which brought with it an influx of the drinking element, including canal boatmen. More important, perhaps, was an element of civic prestige. Playing host to a "unique institution of national importance ... bestowed on its promoters the aura of progressive and enlightened thinking."[20]

There was undoubtedly a profit motive, too: the asylum, promising an influx of patients and their families, some of them wealthy, was a potential boon to the local economy. As Rothman suggests, up-and-coming communities often competed for the chance to have such institutions in their midst, "confident that the resulting income would more than compensate for any nuisance."[21] In imagining such profitable possibilities, Binghamton's leaders were assuming a relatively free intercourse, commercial and otherwise, between the city and the asylum. This assumption, however, proved to be contrary to Turner's intentions—a conflict of expectations that would later erupt in hostilities.

Once a site for the asylum had been selected, Turner hastened to start construction, personally hiring the contractors and begging donations for building materials. Excavation began within a month, masonry work within two; the cornerstone was laid, with solemn ceremony, on 28 September 1858.[22] Despite, or perhaps because of, a constant downpour, the oratory flowed, with dignitaries aplenty lauding the founder's vision and prophesying the immortality of his renown. The speakers included Turner's friend Dr. John W. Francis; Benjamin F. Butler, the Democratic politician (Andrew Jackson's attorney general and Martin Van Buren's secretary of war) who had replaced John D. Wright as president of the board in 1857; and Edward Everett, a heralded orator in his time who is best remembered now—such are the vicissitudes of fame!—for a long-winded speech in 1863 that was then and forever to be overshadowed by the terse eloquence of Lincoln's Gettysburg Address.

On this occasion, neither Everett nor the other speakers held a candle to the Reverend Mr. Bellows, who had also addressed the Broadway Tabernacle meeting in 1855. At Binghamton, Bellows confronted the moral and philosophical implications of the disease concept of inebriety with remarkable clarity and sophistication (see chapter 4).

Defending the Idea

Even as the New York State Inebriate Asylum began to rise, stone upon stone, the battle for funding it carried over into the 1858 legislative session. Now forty-one "aye" votes were cast, still far short of a majority. Opponents of the asylum echoed the conventional attitudes toward inebriety that Turner was so determined to change. In his travels across the state he often encountered "the prejudices of the average citizen who had never for a moment thought of the drunkard as a diseased man needing the medical treatment of a hospital." Such citizens, tarring drunkards and criminals with the same moral brush, "thought that the Inebriate Asylum had originated in the brain of some fanatic, and that the endowment of such a scheme had grown out of the weakness of human nature, the frailty of human judgment, and the absurdity of human action" (*H*, 53).

A rich farmer, for one, could understand "the equity of the dog law which taxes the owner of the good dog to pay for the sheep maimed and destroyed by the bad dog, but could not see the justice of a statute which should tax a traffic for the medical treatment of the disease which that traffic creates." This same man could "not believe the disease theory of drunkenness," which the Bible taught him was a sin (*H*, 48).

A college professor contended that the very existence of the asylum would stimulate intemperance by encouraging the moderate drinker to suppose he might become a drunkard with impunity, since he could always enter the asylum for a cure; the healthy fear of developing inebriety would thus "be entirely removed." Yet another adversary, a jurist, worried that the asylum would undermine the common-law tradition of holding drunkards responsible for their actions. "Having had some experience as a judge in trying all kinds of criminals from the sneak thief to the murderer," he asseverated, "I am convinced that society would be injured by declaring the drunkard an irresponsible being. Three-quarters of the criminals who are tried would enter the plea of inebriety as a defense for their crimes" (*H*, 48–49).[23]

Turner scorned such objections as the sort formerly mounted against the medical treatment of insanity, arguments that had long since been put to shame by Philippe Pinel in France and by other European and American humanitarians: "Twenty years after Pinel's appeal to France in behalf of his humane enterprise, the good people of Massachusetts began to agitate the subject of building an insane asylum. The leading journals of that day opposed the undertaking, arguing that the building of insane asylums would have the tendency to increase lunacy and to multiply crime. Such was the intelligence of the editors of Massachusetts seventy years ago!" (*H,* 49). In order to prove the obsolescence of such thinking–which was indeed obsolete in the context of the prevailing "moral treatment" of the poor, the criminal, and the insane–Turner obtained more than 8,000 signatures in support of public funding for the asylum. Enlightened popular will finally swayed the legislature in 1859: the state would partially underwrite the asylum if every tenth bed were reserved for indigent inebriates.

Early Financial and Political Struggles

Two years later, when the board appealed for increased funding, the resulting bill created a legal conundrum for the asylum's future by seeming, as political opponents feared, to "give the institution a perpetual contract which the legislature of the State of New York could not abrogate or impair." The issue was how to reconcile the state's interests in the private corporation it was financing with those of the board. The twelfth section of the original charter (1854) had promised that the state's empowering act would remain in force for fifty years, "subject, however, to amendment and repeal by the legislature." It had also stated that should the asylum ever be dissolved, its buildings and grounds would be ceded to the State "for some benevolent institution" (*H,* 49–50).

Now, the board pleaded, this provision was impeding its efforts to raise money from rich private investors who wished "to establish free beds to provide an asylum for their inebriate sons," as well as for poor patients. The price of an endowed bed, figured at $5,000, was simply too high unless would-be philanthropists could "be assured that their investments will be perpetual" (*H,* 50–51). So, said the board, the charter's twelfth section must be repealed.

A compromise was reached, but it turned out to be a legal time bomb. The board stipulated that endowed beds could be occupied by indigent patients "when the donor and legator fail to name the said patients to fill the said free beds." In exchange, the state adopted the board's "repealing clause," which read, "All acts and parts of acts inconsistent with this act are hereby repealed." This seemingly simple sentence would cause a hul-labaloo in later years, when Turner and his allies interpreted it as having secured "the property of the corporation forever for the medical treatment of the inebriate," hence preventing the state "from diverting the Hospital to any other use, and the stockholder from the sale of its estate" (*H*, 50–51). Despite its apparent resolution, then, the question of the state's ulti-mate control over the asylum remained open.

Turner's political mettle was tested again the following year, 1862, when a hostile legislator from northern Essex County tried to repeal the asylum's charter. Turner retaliated by invading this foe's home turf and lining up the support of his constituents for a bill "doubling the Asy-lum's portion of the State excise tax on liquor" (which was not, however, adopted.) "The result of the campaign through Essex County," he sarcas-tically recalled, "proved to the honorable member that the people in his district were intensely interested in the Asylum, and the bill for the repeal of its charter was withdrawn by the honorable member from the hands of the committee to whom it was referred" (*H*, 52).

In October 1862, during a lull in the political combat, Turner married Gertrude Middlebrook, daughter of Colonel George Middlebrook, "one of the oldest and most respected citizens" of Wilton, Connecticut (*MA*, 2). Of their courtship, wedding, and ensuing family life almost nothing is known except that Turner's wife and children were used as pawns in his Binghamton disputes.

Turner's honeymoon with the state, meanwhile, abruptly ended. Yet another thrust against the asylum had to be parried in 1863, when the boards of supervisors from several counties conspired against its charter. Turner leaped into the fray once more, flexing his political muscle. With the help of Dr. Valentine Mott, who had accepted the presidency of the board in 1861, he initiated a new petition drive on an unprecedented scale. Along with letters and testimonials from European specialists and from medical superintendents across the United States, Turner garnered the signatures of "sixty leading judges of the State, six hundred lawyers, two thousand physicians, five thousand leading business men and farm-ers"–a bloc representing nearly half the property interests of New York state (*S*, 309). This monster petition effectively put a stop to legislative harassment of the asylum, which throughout the political maneuvering had been, all too slowly, under construction.

The protracted delays had served to fuel the legislative insurgency. Would the building really ever be ready? When would the godly business of saving inebriates actually begin? For although a few patients had been admitted in 1860, the asylum was soon shut down in order to complete construction and did not reopen until June 1864–although it was *still* unfinished, in part because two disastrous fires in less than two months in 1863 had "destroyed the carpentry shop and sash factory, creating an estimated $8,000 worth of damage."[24]

At the root of the delays, however, was the sheer magnitude and expense of the project. For Turner, what would fit the inebriate asylum's loftily spiritual mission was nothing less than a commensurately magnificent material manifestation, conceived on "a palace-like scale" (*MA,* 9) as gargantuan as his petition drive. Turner saw the building as the visible sign of his own heroic vision; from the start he took absolute control of the project, hiring a young but promising carpenter from New York to assist him. This was Isaac G. Perry, who went on to local success as an architect and later designed the New York State Capitol. Perry's job was to translate Turner's exacting specifications into limestone, brick, and mortar.

Design of the Inebriate Asylum

The building plan emanated from Turner's foreign travels, during which he had studied the design of Europe's leading asylums. He must also have contemplated some of the cathedrals, for the style he adopted was Gothic Revival, heavily "castellated" with "massive towers, turrets and buttresses embattled at the top" (*H,* viii). The exterior walls, faced with limestone quarried in nearby Syracuse, were to measure 1,453 feet across the front of five attached buildings. (All the elaborate facing was, alas, removed in 1993 when the building, long in disrepair, began to shed some of its limestone; the rest succumbed to jackhammers.)[25]

In addition to administrative offices and patient quarters–ten wards, each comprising twenty-two rooms of eleven by seventeen feet, with twelve-foot ceilings–the institution would house a lavish array of amenities: a spacious dining hall; a reading room and library with shelving capacity for 20,000 volumes; a chapel with stained-glass windows and seating for five hundred worshippers; a stage for lectures and dramatic entertainments; three expansive reception parlors; lavatories "furnished

The New York State Inebriate Asylum, exterior view. From Turner, *History of the First Inebriate Asylum.*

with all the appliances of the Russian bath"; numerous industrial work-shops as well as diverse recreational facilities, including bowling alleys, a billiard room, and a gymnasium (patients could also go rowing on the river or riding on the grounds); a kitchen and bakery; and a conservatory or winter garden to accommodate 100,000 plants, "which will afford the patients recreation and study, and make for the Asylum a perpetual sum-mer" (*H*, ix)–not a bad idea, considering the long, snowy, and bleakly over-cast winters that are characteristic of upstate New York. The interior ap-pointments were no less sumptuous: "handsome, hand-carved, bilateral oak staircases, wooden half-paneling and cabinetry, and decorative plas-terwork, giving it a resemblance to a high-class saloon"!–or, perhaps more appropriately, to "a first-class hotel."[26] Even the building's infrastructure was state-of-the-art: steam heat, gas lighting, and ducts for enough fan-driven ventilation "to displace the air in the hospital every three minutes" (*H*, viii).

To say the least, nothing about the New York State Inebriate Asylum was done on the cheap, and non-indigent patients paid accordingly: $20 a week in advance for a minimum three-month commitment. (The manda-tory stay was steadily lengthened to one year, once the asylum went into operation.) Valentine Mott boasted that there had been 4,728 applica-tions for admission between 1858 and 1861, including four hundred from women (*H*, 167–68). But whereas even male opium addicts were selec-tively admitted to the asylum, female inebriates were not–a policy that Turner regretted and one for which he compensated in his later efforts to establish a Woman's National Hospital for Inebriates and Opium Eaters in Wilton, Connecticut.

Turner's meticulous plans reflected the asylum movement's preoccu-pation with design as a crucial means to the desired therapeutic end. Rothman shows that "the appropriate arrangement of the asylum, its physical dimensions and daily routine," monopolized the thinking of Tur-ner's psychiatric counterparts, the medical superintendents, for whom "every detail of institutional design was a proper and vital" consideration and whose skills were to be those of the architect and the administrator, not the laboratory technician. This was certainly true of Turner, who left laboratory research behind and whose deepest investment in the asylum seems to have been in its initial planning. He held the same conviction as Thomas Kirkbride, long-time director of the Pennsylvania Hospital for the

Insane and author of an influential 1847 textbook on asylum organization, who believed, says Rothman, that "in settling these technical matters of construction and maintenance, he was confronting and solving the puzzle of curing insanity."[27]

The architecture of the inebriate asylum was generally consistent with that of contemporary insane asylums as described by Rothman: "Typically, a central structure of several stories stood in the middle of the asylum grounds, and from it radiated long and straight wings. The main edifice, and usually the most ornate one, was an administration building, fronted with a columned portico and topped with a cupola of height and distinction." The patient quarters in the wings were ordinarily plainer, with "bare and unrelieved facades" and row upon row of unadorned windows, sometimes giving the appearance of a factory. The "regimented quality of the wing design" jibed, in fact, with the therapeutic premium on "order and regularity": "Its precise divisions, its uniformity and repetitiousness, symbolized superintendents' determination to bring steady discipline into the lives of the insane and to inspire private families to emulation."[28]

The elaborate decoration of the inebriate asylum's entire exterior (not just the central building) and the luxury of its interior appointments marked, however, significant variations from the typical design of insane asylums—suggesting a perception of how the needs of inebriates might differ from those of mental cases. Such opulence made a subtle statement about the essential nature of the inebriate, at least the inebriate of a certain class: that his deviation from social norms was less radical than the madman's. He was not so much a creature of otherness, rendered foreign to polite society by frightening derangement, as a Victorian gentleman in ruins who retained enough shreds of his former dignity still to be recognizable to the sober world and who would recover his respectability amid the comfortingly familiar trappings of a fine home away from home.

This view may suggest that Turner was inclined to treat his patients with kid gloves. Quite the contrary. The severity of his ideas about the asylum's regimen actually conflicted with the benevolence of his design for the building. These strict notions were also informed by orthodox thinking within the asylum movement about optimal conditions for curing insanity. Behind "moral treatment" was the assumption that the root cause of insanity, including the insanity of inebriety, was to be found in the disturbing nature of American society itself. Henry W. Bellows had articulated this idea in his Broadway Tabernacle address in 1855:

> The same stimulus, which makes our commercial and mechanical life of enterprise, and swiftness, which hurries along our railroads and steamships, and devours the wilderness, gives a fearfulness of competition, a recklessness of haste, a fever of the blood and brain to our people, which makes them cravers of strong drinks—vast consumers of rich and exciting food, and of stimulating liquors. Almost all our successful citizens are taxed beyond their strength; are doing two or three men's work, and are tempted to inebriety by their exhaustion, and the necessity of keeping up their spirits to the mark. And then, of course, in this commercial *stampede* there are thousands of disappointed competitors in the race, men weaker in the power of enterprise, but often strongest in sweet and noble endowments, who are trampled beneath the hurrying crowd, and left to solace themselves with whatever they can find to cheer or drown their sorrows.
>
> The drunkenness of this country is almost a part of the national character and policy. It may be almost said to be the measure of the cerebral excitability and working temper of our people. The nation is drunk with youth, the new wine of political freedom and democratic ideas. It is a divine intoxication, having its great providential purpose, and its magnificent results; but it is attended by a fearful shadow—intemperance of speculation, intemperance of feeling, intemperance of appetite. (Quoted in *H*, 64–65)

If insanity was, at least in part, a social disease, then it was logical to seek its cure in creating, as Rothman says, "a different kind of environment, which methodically corrected the deficiencies of the community," including the pathogenic aspects of familial life itself.[29] One of the requirements, therefore, was that the asylum should stand apart from its surroundings. Turner envisioned it as an island fortress to which patients would be strictly confined and from which their families would be strictly excluded. He went so far in 1866 as to petition the legislature for a special police force "to guard the Asylum from without, and to protect its patients within" (*H*, 56). The objection that no other medical facilities in the history of the state had ever requested, let alone received, this degree of security was to no avail. As usual, Turner got his way.

Segregation of inmates from the general population was, in fact, another cardinal principle of the "moral treatment" at insane asylums, although it was often modified in practice in order to pacify the patients' anxious relatives and to satisfy legitimate public curiosity. Medical superintendents, Rothman observes, "dared not seal off the [mental] institution from society." They had to maintain a difficult balance between what was "to the immediate benefit of the individual inmate" and what was in "the long-range interest of mental hospitals in the nation." Because the asylum was a novel institution, it had to remain open to scrutiny at least enough to allay any suspicions about covert inhumane treatment. Otherwise, "legislative appropriations and charitable gifts would be curtailed and families would be loath to commit sick members." It became incumbent upon superintendents to invite outsiders to tour the facilities and to permit brief contact between patients and their families on the condition that the inmates be committed for at least a few months.[30]

Turner, however, rejected any such compromises. That he proved to be adamant on this point would cause him no end of trouble. His insistence on isolating his patients may have derived from his sense of the idiosyncratic nature of the disease he was treating. Not *all* the practices of insane asylums were necessarily applicable to an inebriate asylum, and the singular vulnerability of drunkards to the Demon Rum seemed to demand a quarantine to shield them from temptation. It is not surprising, then, that Turner pressed for a state law, enacted in April 1864, prohibiting "the sale of all kinds of fermented and distilled liquors within one-half a mile of the outward bounds of the lands and premises of the Asylum" and, furthermore, declaring "that no person should pass upon the lands owned by said institution without written authority from one of the officers of said Hospital." The following year a bill was passed making it a misdemeanor to give or sell alcohol, opium, or tobacco to any patient of the asylum; each violation carried a fine of $50 (*H*, 55). Both measures ignored the protests of Binghamton's rum sellers, who complained that it was impossible for them to distinguish inebriate patients (who had snuck out) from their regular clientele.

Attached to both laws was also a provision allowing involuntary commitment of patients by state and county judges for terms of three months (stretched to one year in the 1866 bill). Turner overrode his legislative opponents' concern that this provision "might under some circumstances be an instrument of oppression by confining persons not drunkards in the true meaning of that word without power of redress" (*H*, 55). Ironically, it was Turner himself who would become a victim of oppression he was powerless to redress.

With its main building and one wing nearly completed, the New York

State Inebriate Asylum opened its doors in the summer of 1864. Turner's vision had been triumphantly realized after a quarter-century of untold labor. He would "rather have built the asylum at Binghamton," he liked to say, "than been president of the United States" (*MA*, 19). "The most active interest was manifested all over the State in the work," Crothers attests. Turner was "most enthusiastically praised," recognized as "the great presiding genius" of this pioneering institution. "Pioneers rarely see the result of their labors," Crothers observes. "The great sowers of truth rarely ever see the reapers or harvest" (*S*, 311). But the savor of success turned to ashes in Turner's mouth within months of his installation as the asylum's first superintendent. It would be a very bitter harvest.

3

The Battle of Binghamton

For all the fanfare that preceded it, Dr. J. Edward Turner's reign at the New York State Inebriate Asylum began inauspiciously. In the aftermath of the two fires in 1863, the monumental building still stood incomplete. Then fire struck again, in September 1864, gutting the unfinished north wing; "only a two-hour bucket brigade" spared the south wing.[1] Insurance payments of $81,000 did not cover the loss of stored materials, including flooring, woodwork, and glass for the winter garden. Although Turner was away from Binghamton during the blaze, he and his assistant would later be blamed for setting it.

Of more immediate concern was the revenue flow. Reportedly, thousands of potential patients had applied for admission, but a mere handful actually appeared in 1864. Between February 1865 and February 1866, forty more patients were received, half of whom left within that year, shrinking the overall asylum population to thirty.[2] The medical staff consisted of Turner himself and two assistants: Dr. T. Jefferson Gardiner, whom he had known since boyhood, and Dr. John Hill.

Asylum Patients

A chaplain, Samuel W. Bush, arrived a few months later. In his first official report, which put the best face on the asylum's achievements so far, the chaplain described the patients as "for the most part, persons in middle life, who have occupied important positions in society." Among them were "professional men, well educated, of refined taste, and of decided ability," as well as others with "business abilities of no mean order." Except for two or three men "so demoralized as to render them seemingly indifferent as to what shall be their condition in the future," the rest seemed to be "fitted by their social and amiable qualities to render a home happy and to be an ornament in the circle in which they have hitherto moved." Most had arrived "in a deteriorated condition," Bush continued, one suffering from delirium tremens and another so weak that he required help to alight from the carriage and climb to his room. Nearly without exception, however, all made significant gains within a few weeks or months; some changed markedly for the better. "The feeble become strong; the emaciated muscular; the nervous calm; the sad cheerful; and more or less hopeful in respect to the future." Such results, the chaplain declared, proved the efficacy of Turner's prescriptive routine:

> [A] medicine intended to be adapted to the condition of each patient is daily administered, and the physical condition of each daily scrutinized; alcoholic stimulants, together with opium and tobacco, rigidly excluded; the meals [attendance mandatory] are promptly served at the appointed time; the time for rising and retiring [ten P.M.] is regularly indicated and required to be observed; four hours per day are allotted for exercise in the open air, on ample grounds belonging to the asylum, and abundant provision is made for in-door recreation; religious exercises [also mandatory] are held at fixed times every day, morning and evening, and the usual preaching service on the Sabbath.[5]

Not all patients, it was clear from Turner's part of the same report, were altogether cheerful about the regimen. Understandably, the superintendent wrote, "a man who will abandon home and all the elegancies of life–cast himself adrift from all the social ties which bind him to wife, children, parent, sister and brother, for the purpose of indulging in his *morbid* appetite for alcoholic poison, will, in the hours of his restraint in an hospital, resort to all kinds of deception and misrepresentation for the purpose of working upon the sympathy of family and friends to obtain their consent to his discharge."[4]

For instance, one man of thirty-five (who started drinking when he was ten) had been bribing the family coachman for the keys to the wine cellar. His parents eventually caught on and sent their son to Binghamton among the original cadre of patients. Despite unflagging efforts by Turner and his staff, the man did not improve, and he was pronounced incurable after a year's treatment. The family was advised to commit him permanently; confinement was his last, best hope. But the patient preyed upon his parents' sympathy and won his release. He promptly took up the bottle and terrorized his family, which returned him to the asylum. Yet five months later his mother was pleading again for his deliverance.

> We replied that her son had been sent to the asylum by an order of the court, under the affidavits of two physicians and two freeholders, which declared that he had lost self-control, and was, from his dipsomania, dangerous to remain at large. Under such circumstances the institution could not take the responsibility of discharging him. Further, that if her son was discharged, and should return home and have delirium tremens (to which he was pre-disposed), and under this condition of mind and body should commit murder, *we* should be responsible to the community for the crime. The parent has no more right to turn upon society the dipsomaniac son than he has to unlock the doors of our insane asylums and let loose upon the community the madman, or give to the suicidal maniac a pistol or a knife for self destruction.[5]

Some patients, although searched for contraband upon entrance to the asylum, showed remarkable ingenuity in outwitting the authorities, such as by concealing a flask somewhere on the grounds.[6] Others took drastic measures to escape confinement. There was one such incident on 16 September 1865, at one o'clock in the morning. A night watchman, William A. Wilson, was minding his business ("being engaged in reading and sitting in a chair") when he was attacked by two inmates, Samuel Gilman and H. C. Smith, who stuffed a handkerchief in his mouth, wrapped his arms around his body, forced him upstairs, and lashed him to a bed. Under suspicion himself, Wilson at first expostulated that he had never bought any tobacco or liquor for patients, or written any letters for them, or smuggled any correspondence in or out. Upon further interrogation, he confessed that he *had* supplied tobacco to several inmates (whom he named) and, furthermore, that he had "voluntarily submitted to the above treatment from said Gilman and Smith in order that they might be enabled to escape by his submission from said Inebriate Asylum."[7]

As Wilson's statement implies, patients' mail was carefully monitored. They could receive letters, but they were not given stamps to send any out, and they were forbidden receipt of uninspected packages. The escape plan of Gilman and Smith took account of another asylum practice: the patient population was counted twice daily. The pair must have waited to make their move until after the regular nightly bed check. They could not simply have climbed out a window, because those on the lower ward were barred with iron grates.

Such treachery undoubtedly reinforced Turner's beliefs about discipline and security at the asylum. Not only did keeping a tight rein on patients and staff agree with asylum movement principles for "moral treatment," but the policy also suited the stern rigidity of Turner's personality. "In the early part of his career he was critical and sharp in his judgment of men and events," his friend T. D. Crothers acknowledges. "Later he became broader and more charitable in his view and opinions" (*MA*, 3). "Later," we suppose, came after Turner's tenure at Binghamton. While there, he bristled with an air of command, combined with a stolid remoteness that rubbed people the wrong way.

Even Crothers, who worshiped him, concedes that Turner was "neither a politician or diplomat" and recognizes that his manner was often inscrutable: "There was a superior outlook and daring energy which pressed the thought with a positiveness that could not be mistaken. To strangers there was something mysterious in the loftiness of his mental ambition and purpose, which was interpreted in various ways according to the discernment of the person" (*MA*, 13, 15). Insofar as others discerned Turner to be grasping and arrogant, the same qualities that had enabled him to attain his dream of founding the inebriate asylum now became liabilities in managing it. Inevitably, conflicts erupted among the superintendent, the patients, the board, and the Binghamton community.

In 1879, when the New York State Inebriate Asylum was closed, one observer wisely reflected on its "chequered career," attributing the early blunders to the experimental stage of the enterprise: "The hospital has been a school; the patients have been teachers."[8] If the asylum was a school, then Turner, whose practical experience as a physician was slight at best and whose administrative experience was nil, proved to be stubbornly unteachable. He could not easily believe he had anything to learn from his patients, with whom he had differences of both philosophy and class background. A submerged theme throughout Turner's troubles in Binghamton was the dubiousness of his social as well as his medical credentials. On both counts he was found wanting by his supposed superiors, including some of the very patients over whom he was lording his authority.

The proportion of indigent inebriates at the asylum, never high, was especially low at the outset. As Crothers notes, the first patients were predominantly "from the wealthy and influential families of the country and after the first glamor was over and they had become somewhat restored they began to rebel against restraint, the methods of management" (*MA*, 9). Like the young man Turner described in his 1866 report, they complained to relatives and other outsiders about conditions within the asylum and harsh treatment from a superintendent who was less than a true gentleman. "Some were tactless enough to ask what had become of the elegancies by which they had been lured: Where were the blooming conservatories, the blooded horses, the Russian and Turkish baths? They complained that, besides being treated like criminals, the patients were barely warmed and only poorly fed."[9]

Dr. Willard Parker and the Asylum Board

Matters came to a crisis when Valentine Mott, a Turner ally, died in April 1865, and Dr. Willard Parker was elected to replace him as head of the asylum's board of directors. For this turn of events, ironically, Turner himself was largely responsible: he had recommended Parker for the job, believing him to be "a physician well equipped to make an able President" (*H*, 233). Mott had been a hard-liner on discipline, united with Turner in "his profound contempt for the plan of relying upon a drunkard's honor and pledge" (*H*, 170). By and large, Turner had always enjoyed the acquiescence of the board in running the asylum as he saw fit. The new president, however, was disposed to interfere.

Born in Lyndeborough, New Hampshire, in 1800, educated at Harvard and Princeton, Willard Parker was "one of the most eminent American physicians of the nineteenth century," famous at an early age for his innovations in surgery (a pioneer in treating aneurisms surgically, he later became "the first American doctor to successfully remove an abscessed appendix").[10] In 1839, Parker was appointed to a professorship at the prestigious College of Physicians and Surgeons in New York City. He became highly visible both for his medical accomplishments and for his advocacy of public health and temperance reform. As one of the founders, in 1870, of the American Association for the Cure of Inebriety, Parker was instrumental in disseminating and legitimating the idea of chronic drunkenness as a disease. He was, it seemed, the ideal candidate for president of the asylum's board.[11]

Parker first visited Binghamton in August 1865 and observed the asylum's operations for two days. He had lots of questions for the superintendent, some of them probing. How many patients were being treated? How many had died? Did the income from inmates exceed the expenditures? Then, as Turner remembered, Parker showed his hand, stating that "he was very sorry to see the patients laboring under so much mental irritation, and that he would suggest their having a larger liberty and their being placed upon their honor, as they were all gentlemen belonging to Christian households." This, Parker added, was "the only plan which can make the Asylum popular with the patients." Turner replied at length that

> the mental disturbance of the patient proceeded from the morbid conditions of the brain and stomach, and that his surroundings did not in any way enter into the physical causes of his disease; that he [Parker] should remember that among the patients under treatment in the Asylum were homicidal and suicidal dipsomaniacs, thieves and liars, the destroyers of homes and violators of the marriage vows, and that all of these mental, social and criminal conditions were the effects of a physical disease as much as delirium in typhus fever; that no better illustration of the utter loss of self-control in the inebriate, and the price he will pay for a single drink is afforded than in the story related by Professor Mussey, of Cincinnati. "A few years ago," said the professor, "a tippler was put into the almshouse in Massachusetts. Within a few days he devised numerous expedients to procure rum, but failed. At length, however, he hit upon one which was successful. He went into the wood-yard of the establishment, and placing one hand upon a block and with an axe in the other, he struck it off at a single blow. With the stump raised and streaming he ran into the house, and cried 'Get some rum, get some rum, my hand is off.' In the confusion and bustle of the occasion a bowl of rum was brought, into which he plunged the bleeding member of his body, then raised the bowl to his mouth, drinking freely, and exclaimed, 'I am satisfied.'" (*H*, 233–34)

This exchange could not have reassured Parker, who was, reasonably, worried about the gap between the asylum's huge capacity and its small patient count.[12] Turner's crude and bloody anecdote may also have offended Parker's refined sensibilities. There was, in any event, no mistaking Turner's resistance to coddling inebriates, whatever their familial and religious pedigrees; he admitted no distinctions in rank among dipsomaniacs.

In Parker's view, however, making the asylum more popular, and thus more prosperous, was inseparable from making it far less regimented. The institution's interests lay in attracting precisely those privileged patients who would least tolerate Turner's draconian rules, which they would regard both as an abrogation of their right to life, liberty, and the pursuit of alcohol and as an affront to their gentlemanly honor. From this point on, the Battle of Binghamton was joined.

It wasn't that Parker completely discounted the need for medical control. It was a matter of degree in imposing discipline and of discretion in its application. Writing about the asylum's history at the time of its dissolution in 1879, Parker raised the same issues that had worried Turner in 1865:

> Questions of discipline and treatment arose: should half-crazed patients be restrained and controlled, or should they be left to themselves, to seek the means of intoxication when the excess of appetite was upon them? And if they rebelled against medical treatment could they be compelled to submit, these men who had come there of their own freewill? Above all, what employment could be found for a set of idle men, many of them men of ability, of intelligence, of power, except for this unfortunate appetite?
>
> All these questions might have been met, if not solved, in a small institution, sustained by a wise legislation–for *authority* seems to be a necessity in the management–until experience should have been gained for the needed increase in numbers and accommodation. . . .
>
> Of course the money which would have built and equipped a small asylum was all expended on this immense shell, and further grants were needed to put even a part in good condition. There are also changes in the management made necessary by the difficulty of finding any man possessed of the needed qualifications–and they are many–who would be willing to take such a thankless post. The highest medical qualifications to treat disease, the patience and faith of a Christian and the firmness and courage of a State-prison warden are all required.[13]

It may be that Parker's views had gravitated closer to Turner's by 1879, after years of disappointments in the administration of the asylum. Turner was not the only superintendent, as it happened, who could not walk on water. Still, Parker was being mainly consistent with what he had earlier said.

In an affidavit dated 16 April 1868, Parker gave his own partisan version of that fateful visit to the asylum in 1865:

> The patients were in a state of discontent and antagonism with said Turner acting as Superintendent of the Asylum, and who claimed to have entire control. They complained that the Superintendent was a man of violent and ungovernable temper; that he cared only for their money, which was payable in advance; that his conduct toward and treatment of them seemed to have but the single purpose to drive them away; that instead of being kind and courteous in his intercourse, he was rude and overbearing, resorting not infrequently to personal violence. Upon this, his first visit, he [Parker] was thoroughly convinced that if the institution was ever to prove a success, a change in its management was absolutely necessary.[14]

It is difficult to assess the validity of these accusations, especially Turner's alleged propensity to "personal violence"—whether of a physical or merely a verbal sort is unclear. It *was* common practice within the asylum movement for patients to pay several months in advance, as a check against their leaving prematurely; so much for Turner's alleged greed. Parker's portrait of him is otherwise recognizable, if exaggerated, in its delineation of the superintendent's irascibility and his fetish for absolute control.

The Fight for Control of the Asylum

Turner had to go, and Parker tried to ease him out as gently as possible. First he maneuvered for control of the board, inducing many of Turner's friends to resign—by inconveniently requiring their attendance at all future meetings—and then replacing them with his own allies. In the annual meeting of 6 June 1866 the purge was accomplished, and Parker temporarily gained the upper hand: Turner was to be offered a buy-out. Predictably, he balked at the idea, lamenting that "he had never anticipated that the gentlemen whom he had invited to co-operate with him in building the Asylum, would have mutinied against their host; such a proceeding would have put to blush the banditti of Italy" (*H*, 239).

Parker then took a different tack, professing concern about Turner's health. The superintendent was looking rather peaked, was he not?—understandably exhausted by his noble labors. Maybe he and his family needed a vacation—a long vacation. The board would be pleased, in recognition of the superintendent's long and selfless service, to underwrite a two-year European furlough. When Turner still demurred, insisting that he would not leave his post under any circumstances, the tactics for expelling him became nastier. As he recalled, even the furlough proposal had been accompanied by a threat from Ausburn Birdsall, one of the hostile local trustees: "If you do not accept this offer we have determined to drive you out of the Institution, and to disgrace you" (*H*, 241).

On 25 June 1866, one day after the superintendent had refused to cooperate, he was summarily fired. Hoping to rally his supporters, Turner took the midnight train for New York (his enemies accused him of also spiriting away the asylum's records). Having arranged for a special meeting of the board, Turner returned to Binghamton, where Dr. Hill had been placed temporarily in charge with orders "to put the patients upon their honor, and to permit them to go and come at pleasure" (*H*, 241). Turner met with the president of the board for the last time, to demand Parker's own resignation, insulting him to his face by blasting his lenient policy as "even more absurd and insane" than that of the demented Dr. Darling Goodfellow, whose similar desire to make his hospital popular with patients had led him to substitute mind-cure for the scalpel and to advertise "surgery without a knife" (*H*, 241). Parker was unmoved.

On 10 July 1866 the special session of the board was packed with trustees loyal to Turner, and he was promptly reinstated, on the grounds that his dismissal had been a violation of the corporation's charter. Committees were then appointed to audit the asylum's books and to investigate any charges against the superintendent. None, in fact, was formally filed, although Parker and his allies had begun a whispering campaign, insinuating that they preferred not to embarrass Turner by publicly disclosing his offenses.

In reaction to this defeat, Parker played his trump card. At the next board meeting, on 11 September 1866, his supporters resolved that all current construction at the asylum was to cease and all remaining inmates (about a dozen) were to be discharged as of 1 October; the institution was then to be closed until the building was properly "completed for the reception of patients" (*H*, 251). As Turner recognized, this was an attempt to starve him out. Supplies to the asylum were stopped, including even the milk and butter ordinarily delivered by the resident farmer. Turner's wife pleaded with the man, to no avail, "that her young children had been using the milk of one cow, and that a change might make the babies sick and endanger their lives."[15] In a polemically maudlin passage in his *History,*

Turner recalled that a neighbor, a survivor of similarly fiendish tactics in her native Ireland, had taken pity on his starving babes and twice a day had carried them a pail of milk on her head, all the while cursing Birdsall (Parker's henchman) as the kind of monster her village priest had once described as "born with a dead soul in him" (*H*, 252–53).

Ausburn Birdsall was a Binghamton lawyer who, according to Senta Rypins, "soon shouldered himself into a position of power. Eventually the conflict narrowed down to a duel between Birdsall and Turner."[16] Turner had had legal dealings with Birdsall as early as January 1865, when the lawyer sold him some of his own land for development as a farm. When Birdsall was elected a trustee later that year, one alarmed citizen was moved to object: "I have been told that Mr. B. bribed some high functionary at Washington to secure his appointment as Naval Officer of the Port of New York. A man who would commit so great a crime as to bribe an officer of the United States is not a propper [*sic*] person to be a trustee of the Inebriate Asylum."[17]

Charges of Arson

Parker, meanwhile, renewed his efforts to dominate the board by revealing specific charges against Turner at the meeting of 17 October 1866. One of the superintendent's friends was shocked to hear the venomous bill of particulars from anti-Turner trustees: "One stated that the founder had set the building on fire [in September 1864], and that there was already positive evidence of his guilt. Another said that he was an embezzler; another, that he was a defaulter; another, that he was a thief; another, that he was a bigamist; another, that he was utterly unfit to manage the Asylum." It seemed too incredible to believe "that a rational human being would work an entire lifetime to found and build a pioneer hospital, and then destroy it by fire, unless that human being was a parricide and utterly irresponsible" (*H*, 255). But this and all the other charges stuck to Turner for the rest of his life.[18]

It may well be true that Turner was temperamentally unsuited to serve as superintendent of the asylum, but his unfitness had nothing to do with the alleged iniquities. The charge of bigamy, for instance, derived from a slanderous story—a complete fabrication—that Turner was really an English adventurer who had abandoned his family in the old world to seek his illicit fortune in the new one. The other charges, equally base, also proved baseless. The accusation of arson was leveled by Parker and his Binghamton confederates only when it became clear that they could not otherwise dislodge the entrenched superintendent. During the summer of 1866, according to Turner, they approached a former patient of the asylum and urged him to complain before the U.S. District Court that the superintendent had illegally opened his mail. When the man refused, the plotters instead induced two men, James Brown and a Mr. McKiver, "to go before the Grand Jury of Broome Co., and swear out an indictment for arson against the founder" (*H*, 263).

Such indictments against Turner and his alleged co-conspirator, Dr. Gardiner, were obtained on 20 September 1866, and Turner was arrested. When he made bail, the bondsman was threatened by a prominent citizen, John Clapp, who predicted that the accused would likely skip town. Turner reported that "Mr. Clapp often expressed himself as convinced of the founder's guilt, and this conviction he entertained long after his acquittal. Mr. Clapp's conviction largely represented public opinion in Binghamton, and the thorough work of the ring in this direction is illustrated by the fact that even the wife of Judge Balcom, who subsequently tried the case, was thoroughly enlisted in the work of defaming the writer. This lady, meeting an old friend, informed him that the man who built the Asylum had had it insured, and had received from the insurance companies $81,000, which he had appropriated to his own use" (*H*, 264). This, then, was Turner's supposed motive for arson: to embezzle the insurance money because he was at risk of defaulting on the asylum's bonds. There was no evidence to support this scenario. The asylum's finances were shown, by the board's own investigatory committee, to be perfectly in order; all but two cents were fully accounted for.

The arson indictment against Turner was ultimately quashed, even before any trial took place. Gardiner's case was heard first (a year later, after a change of venue had been denied), and he was acquitted after only five minutes of jury deliberation! The prosecution's case was exceedingly weak, based as it was on the testimony of "a colored employee [*sic*] of the asylum ... to the effect that he, Brown, had overheard a conversation, carried on in a usual tone of voice, between Drs. Turner and Gardner [*sic*], in which said Turner had instructed said Gardner to burn down the Asylum, as the bonds of the institution had become due; during the said con-

versation they, Drs. Turner and Gardner being at the head of the basement stairs, and he, Brown, at the foot of said stairs" (*H,* 267). McKiver, a
plasterer, further testified that "he had found several barrels of shavings
saturated with linseed oil in the north wing of the Asylum, and that
Dr. Gardner discharged him on the afternoon of the fire" (*H,* 268).

The defense successfully explained the oil-soaked shavings as the
clumsy attempt of a painter's assistant to mop up a spill and then to conceal the accident by stashing the evidence in the north wing. McKiver was
shown to have been too drunk to work on the day he was fired. An insurance executive testified that he had persuaded the reluctant superintendent to buy a fire policy in the first place (in the amount of $300,000), and
an asylum trustee added that he had threatened to resign if Turner did not
take this prudent step.

As for Brown, whose race alone disadvantaged him as a credible witness before a white jury, it was established that on the night of the fire he
"had stated to seven different men that Dr. Turner would be crazy when
he learned of the fire; and that he also told these same men that a patient
named Moulton had threatened to burn the Asylum, and that he, Brown,
believed that Moulton was the guilty party" (*H,* 268). It was suggested,
moreover, that it would have been impossible, given the acoustics of the
building, for Brown to have overheard the damning conversation between
Turner and Gardiner from the bottom of the basement stairs.

The inescapable conclusion was that Brown had been bribed to perjure
himself. Turner had no doubt by whom. He later reported some remarks
made to a third party by Dr. Daniel G. Dodge, one of his successors as
superintendent: "I have, said Dr. Dodge, a colored man named Brown in
the employ of the Asylum who has given me much trouble, and I have
been compelled to discharge him twice, but he has been re-instated by
Dr. Parker. He is the man whose testimony indicted the founder of the
Asylum. He often amuses the patients by relating stories of villainy con-
nected with the Asylum, of which he ought to be ashamed, and yet this
colored man has today more influence with Dr. Parker than any officer of
the institution" (quoted in *H,* 427–28).

Parker and his allies never swallowed their defeat in court; and because they controlled the publicity surrounding the controversy, they kept
their version of events in circulation long after they had finally driven
Turner out of town (although not riding the rail they would have liked to

see him straddling, preferably tarred and feathered). Hence, the prevailing opinion in Binghamton remained that the wily and corrupt superintendent had gotten away with arson and a whole lot more. William E. Dodge, a trustee who had once been persuaded to oppose Turner but later regretted this as "a great mistake on my part," confided to him the opinion of one prominent Binghamtonian "that public sentiment had been so manipulated that *it* had already convicted the founder of a heinous crime, and that there were scarcely fifty persons in the city of Binghamton who believed him innocent" (*H*, 410, 413). Turner–who had neither social nor political standing in the city and who never made friends there (only enemies)–stood continually convicted in the local and national press.

The Asylum and the National Press

The deepest cut, which permanently damaged Turner's reputation, was inflicted by an October 1868 article in the *Atlantic Monthly*, the most influential magazine in America at the time. Written by James Parton, a respected biographer and man of letters, "Inebriate Asylums, and a Visit to One" offered cultivated readers an engaging and comprehensive look at this new social phenomenon, using Binghamton as the focal point. During Parton's sojourn there his ear had been filled with anti-Turner propaganda, much of which he reported as gospel but without ever naming the supposed felon (and thus protecting himself against a defamation suit– a wise move for the author, given the article's high quotient of error, distortion, and slander).[19]

> Fifteen or twenty years ago, an English adventurer living in the city of New York, calling himself a doctor, and professing to treat unnamable diseases, thought he saw in this notion of an Inebriate Asylum (then much spoken of) a chance for feathering his nest. He entered upon the enterprise without delay, and he displayed a good deal of nervous energy in getting the charter, collecting money, and erecting the building. The people of Binghamton, misled by his representations, gave a farm of two hundred and fifty-two acres for the future inmates to cultivate, which was two hundred acres too much; and to this tract farms still more superfluous have been added, until the Asylum estate contains more than five hundred acres. An edifice was begun on the scale of an imperial palace, which will have cost, by the time it is finished and furnished, a million dollars. The restless man pervaded the State raising money, and creating public opinion in favor of the institution. For several years he was regarded as one of the great originating philan-

thropists of the age; and this the more because he always gave out that he was laboring in the cause from pure love of the inebriate, and received no compensation.

Following the anti-Turner line uncritically, Parton went onto expose Turner's alleged schemes and to praise "the most arduous exertions of a public-spirited board of trustees, headed by Dr. Willard Parker" for finally exposing the villain and thwarting a "bold game" that had come too "near succeeding." He insinuated that the adventurer had unjustly beaten the rap for arson, "a crime which is easy to commit, and hard to prove": "Binghamton convicted the prisoner, but the jury was obliged to acquit him." He asserted, moreover, that "the man and his confederates must have carried off an enormous booty."

Again echoing Parker, Parton then assassinated Turner's character: "Ignorant, obstinate, passionate, fussy, and false,–plausible and obsequious at Albany, a violent despot at the Asylum,–he was, of all the people in the world, the precisely worst man to conduct an experiment so novel, and so abounding in difficulties." His "real object," it seemed, was to collect advance payments from a patient and then "to starve and madden him into a sudden departure." Even his name for the institution was all wrong. The foolish term "inebriate asylum," had been "the greatest single obstacle to its growth" by dint of its "affixing a stigma to the unfortunate men who had honored themselves by making so gallant an effort at self-recovery." But let the man and his misdeeds pass into oblivion, Parton concluded. "There never yet was a bad man who was not, upon the whole, a very stupid ass."[20]

There was to be, however, no forgetting or forgiving for Turner; the scandal pursued him to the grave.

Innocence and Exile

How can such enduring animosity be explained in the face of Gardiner's easy acquittal and other indications of Turner's innocence? For one thing, his enemies had come to loath him personally with a hatred so violent that it defied sense in the case of Willard Parker, whose vindictiveness was completely out of character with his reputation for grace and integrity. Parker, who lived in New York, had limited face-to-face dealings with Turner, after all. The malice of Birdsall and others in Binghamton was more clearly motivated: they envied and resented what they took to be Turner's imperious rule of the asylum for which the city had given the land. He "assumes and exercises supreme control," they complained in the 1867 annual report, "and allows no interference, at least on the part of the resident trustees," whom he never consults or even informs about his intentions. Meanwhile, he lives with seignorial arrogance, dispensing "hospitality or charity to his kindred with as much freedom and unreserve as if he owned everything and had unlimited means at his command. In fact, incredible as it may seem, he claims that he is virtually the owner of the institution."[21]

For another thing, Turner refused to let matters rest after 1866. The Battle of Binghamton never truly ended while Turner was still alive to keep fighting it and thus to provoke endless rounds of recrimination. Convinced by his friends that reinstatement was impossible and that the uproar might result in the permanent closure of the asylum, Turner yielded so far as to resign as superintendent in January 1867. But he continued to contend for control of the board, which Parker captured once and for all later in 1867 by means of shady and possibly illegal manipulations of trustee votes and proxies. Turner accepted a severance settlement of $35,000 ($10,000 at once, the balance upon his leaving town): a sum considered extortionate by the board but one that Turner deemed less than fair.[22]

Even in exile, Turner kept the asylum under surveillance, taking note of every failure under the administration of Parker and his allies. He also continued to solicit funds. After yet another fire in March 1870, "he spent three years raising $30,000 to cover the costs of reconstruction, which the insurance company would not cover due to irregularities."[23] This was not a disinterested gesture; Turner still expected to regain his grip on the asylum. "I feel that I would make any [and] all sacrifices to accomplish the work of reorganizing the Asylum and to raise a fund of a million of dollars to endow it," he wrote to his mother in 1873. "This task will finish my life work. The dreams of my childhood the labor of my manhood will be fully realized when this work is consummated."[24]

All the while, Turner launched a steady barrage of criticism against Parker while he contrived to corner the corporate stock, in preparation for a legal assault on his enemies. In fact, over 95 percent of the original asylum stock was transferred from other trustees to Turner, "making him the legal owner of the institution" (*MA*, 10). Turner then filed suit against the rogue trustees in 1876, but the decision of the United States Circuit Court went against him, on a technicality, and he lacked the funds to pursue an appeal. "He refused offers of help on a contingency basis," Rypins reports, "because he had developed an almost paranoid suspiciousness and feared a new conspiracy against him. To the last he was upheld by the certainty that he would yet be able to reopen the case and win the decision. Then, what a triumphant vindication and reinstatement!"[25]

He was beaten decisively in 1879, when the asylum was sold out from under the original corporation to the state of New York for one dollar. Turner and many others considered the transaction flagrantly illegal: a pocket-lining power grab by Parker and his cronies (in cahoots with the infamous William "Boss" Tweed, who had in fact briefly served as a trustee). This was an act, spluttered Turner, "so utterly inconsistent with the provisions of the constitution of the United States, that not a judge or a lawyer who resided outside of the State of New York could be found who believed that such an outrage could have been perpetrated in collusion with the officers of a great State" (*H*, 325). But facing prolonged and possibly futile litigation, Turner decided instead to devote himself to the founding of another pioneering institution, the National Woman's Hospital for Inebriates and Opium Eaters in Wilton, Connecticut (his wife's hometown, to which the Turners had retreated in 1867).[26]

A Second Failure

Turner the tireless warrior rearmed for yet another struggle, canvassing twelve states in quest of support and subscriptions. The new capital campaign was virtually identical to the old one on behalf of the Binghamton asylum. Turner paid 120,000 calls, by his own count, failing to be heard by "more than eleven hundred influential men who were too busy to be interrupted or too rich to be annoyed. He found himself turned from their doors as a beggar, or driven from their premises by their dogs as a tramp, and under all these circumstances, unpleasant or pleasant as they were, he was only bitten six times by their canine defenders" (*H*, 460).

In 1881, however, a charter was granted, and preparations began for groundbreaking on 27 October. As before, elaborate building plans were drawn up, under the direction of an architect, Thomas R. Jackson. Also as before, Turner never rested from his fund-raising labors. There was one important difference, however. The donors of the land—one of whom was

Turner himself[27]–stipulated not only that the hospital should be forever used exclusively for the medical treatment of female inebriates and opium addicts but also that the founding corporation "should not receive any appropriations or gifts from the State of Connecticut," so as "to prevent the manipulation of the institution by politicians."[28] "Never again!" Turner must often have thought. The horrors at Binghamton must never happen again.

Then, four years later, while he was on the road in Ohio to sign up more subscribers, Turner's past caught up with him: Vincent Collyer, a representative to the Connecticut legislature from Darien, recirculated Parton's 1868 *Atlantic Monthly* article among his colleagues and demolished Turner's base of political support.[29] In 1885 a repeal of the charter was unanimously passed by both houses and sent to the governor, who returned the bill to committee in order to give Turner an opportunity to defend himself. As he tells it in a poignant passage from the *History*, he never really stood a chance:

> The writer appeared before this Committee, and stated that the minds of the legislators had been poisoned against the Hospital by Mr. Parton's article and Mr. Collyer's statements, and that he wished to give his version of Dr. Parker's connection with the Asylum at Binghamton; but the chairman, Senator R. J. Walsh, would not allow the history to be given from the writer's stand-point. The senator's manner and talk seemed to be imbued with Dr. Parker's spirit.[30]
>
> One of the Committee asked the writer if he had not been indicted for arson. He answered, "Yes," and then wished to explain, but this privilege was denied him by Senator Walsh.
>
> The Committee the second time unanimously reported for the repeal of the charter, declaring, substantially, that the writer was a very bad man, and that he had only procured this charter for fraudulent purposes. Not a vote in either house was recorded against the repeal. (*H*, 482)

Turner's account of this hearing is largely substantiated by the stenographer's official transcript of the proceedings: when he tried to explain his past, he was rudely shut up. Here, for example, is the exchange about the arson charges:

> MR. MOREHOUSE: I would like to ask the gentleman if he was not indicted for firing the wing of that building at Binghamton and was placed under a bond of $5,000?

DR. TURNER: Now, that opens the question which I would be very happy to present to the Committee.

THE CHAIRMAN: I will ask the gentleman one question in this connection. If you were so indicted, was there a conviction?

DR. TURNER: No, sir. We found–

THE CHAIRMAN: We had better not go into that.

At the end of the hearing, the witness was once again silenced:

DR. TURNER: You won't go back to the Binghamton Asylum.

THE CHAIRMAN: Not at all.

DR. TURNER: I want to give a history of that, and my connection with it and state how that article to which Mr. Morehouse refers came to be written. . . .

THE CHAIRMAN: I do not believe it is necessary to go into that.

DR. TURNER: As the gentleman spoke of that, I wish to show you the character of the stockholders at Binghamton.

THE CHAIRMAN: We don't care anything about that, Doctor.

DR. TURNER: It only shows the class of names I secured in connection with the Binghamton Asylum.

THE CHAIRMAN: I don't think anything has been raised here that affects your standing before this Committee.[31]

The Parton article was indeed adduced as good reason to distrust Turner's intentions. What Turner omitted from his account, however, was that one reason given for the charter repeal was the evident lack of progress in building the National Woman's Hospital. Hostile legislators harped on the fact that nothing had been accomplished since the groundbreaking four years before. They suspected a ruse. As one senator put it, less than grammatically: "And, looking the ground thoroughly over there, the united feeling of the people in the town of Wilton was, Mr. Chairman, that this thing looked too much like a 'skin' for it to run any longer."

"After the first shock of disappointment," Crothers recalls of Turner, "new plans were formed and arrangements for a stock company and a continuation of the building was perfected. Like the elder Napoleon he never recognized defeat and, while driven back and forced to take a new course, his interest and determination were increased" (*MA*, 11–12). To bring his case before the public, in the hope of reviving the National Woman's Hospital project, Turner self-published his *History of the First Inebriate Asylum in the World* (1888). He would survive its appearance by

only a year, during which he insisted that "he was nearer the consumma-
tion of his life purpose than ever before" (*MA,* 12). Just before his death on
24 July 1889, from a severe attack of nephritis, Turner was still making
plans "to bring suit against the State of New York."[32]

The Verdict on Turner

If Turner *had* brought his suit, the Furies would no doubt have continued
to pursue him. As late as 1907, all the old slanders were raked up again by
a story in the *Rochester Union,* against which Turner's widow bitterly pro-
tested.[33] Her husband, it seemed, would rest in peace only when he came
to rest in obscurity. Fortunately, she lived to witness one small affirmation
of Turner's life: in 1909, twenty years after his death, an imposing shaft
was erected on his previously unmarked grave in the Wilton cemetery.
Sponsored by the American Society for the Study of Alcohol and Other
Narcotics, the monument bore this inscription: "The first physician to put
into practical operation the treatment of inebriety as a disease. By the
methods he instituted, thousands have been redeemed, humanity blessed
and the principles of Christianity advanced."[34]

Crothers also made it his business to honor Turner and his achievements, even though acknowledging the man's personal shortcomings.
Crothers implied, for instance, that the National Woman's Hospital might
have become a reality if only Turner had overcome his distrust of others–
including those who offered him generous financial support, but at the
cost of diminishing his absolute power over the project. "The bitter experience at Binghamton impressed him with a lurid fear of its repetition and
while he planned a board for the asylum at Wilton and arranged all the details, he was to have central authority and control" (*MA,* 17). In the end,
Turner's character proved to be as self-defeating in Connecticut as it had
been in New York. In a sense, the National Woman's Hospital was another,
belated victim of the Battle of Binghamton.

That battle was rehearsed in Turner's *History,* his final bid for vindication, in which he presented voluminous evidence in his own defense and
spared not his enemies, especially Parker.[35] What he also did, however,
was to quote them at length and to lay out their allegations forthrightly,
along with pertinent pieces of the public record. Beginning with its gran-
diose title, the *History of the First Inebriate Asylum in the World* was, to be

sure, a pompous performance. "It survives today as a curiosity of literature," says Rypins. "It is no history in any recognizable sense, but a farrago of argument and explanation, interlarded with temperance tracts and case histories, quoted comments and opinions, disjointed reports of the asylum and of the controversy with Parker and Birdsall."[36] Despite its quirkiness, there is nevertheless a disarming candor and a winning scrupulosity about this book that make it hard for disinterested readers to escape the conclusion that Turner was smeared, that he was really not guilty of arson and the rest. The man's prickly personality, which evoked the enmity of some contemporaries, gives forth, on paper, an air of elemental dignity and honesty.

No doubt, Turner wished to make just such an impression. He quotes his old friend Reuben Hyde Walworth as saying, "The history of the Asylum must be written . . . and no one can accomplish that work so well as yourself." Such a history, Walworth added, "will expose the most wicked and cruel conspiracy ever enacted in the growth of any institution, and 'stranger than fiction' will be the verdict of the reader" (*H*, 157). Some might argue that Turner's *History* seems stranger than fiction because it *is* largely fiction, that this elaborate brief for his innocence is really the crowning example of his self-serving genius for mendacity. We think otherwise, pending the discovery of convincing evidence to the contrary.

Aside from any verdict on Turner's guilt or innocence, there remains the historical significance of the Battle of Binghamton. To understand what happened during the brief life of the New York State Inebriate Asylum is to have a microcosmic view of the complex Victorian debate on the nature and treatment of drunkards. The origins of this debate lay, as did the origins of Turner's dream, in the Washingtonian movement of the 1840s. It was the wondrous spectacle of drunkards helping each other to get sober that first made it plausible to suppose that inebriates could under *any* circumstances overcome their consuming appetite. Before the Washingtonians, the strategy of mainstream temperance leaders had been to write off chronic drunkards as hopelessly past saving and therefore not worth the trouble of assisting. They believed that the cure for inebriety lay in its prevention: primarily by smashing the myth of "moderate" drinking, which many temperance advocates envisioned (see the famous Currier lithograph *The Drunkard's Progress*) as merely a way station on the road to inevitable doom and death.

The Washingtonians had inspired the hope that sparked a reformation in the treatment of inebriates. But the egalitarian and compassionate spirit of Washingtonianism ran contrary to the hierarchical and dispassionate spirit of Turner's regime. What was ultimately at stake in the quarrels between the founder and his adversaries was a difference in the conception of drunkards and drunkenness, the conflict between incompatible models of inebriety: one essentially medical, the other essentially moral. Once Turner had been driven from the asylum, the medical regime was supplanted by the moral approach advocated by Parker and first put into play by Turner's successor as superintendent. This man, who had been the moving spirit of the Washingtonian Home in Boston over the preceding decade, was Albert Day.

4

The Asylum's New Day and Its Twilight

In an article on 7 May 1868 the *Binghamton Democrat* celebrated the first year of Albert Day's service as superintendent of the New York State Inebriate Asylum. The paper recalled how the institution had been closed, "owing to the mismanagement of Mr. J. Edward Turner," and then reopened seven months later after "long and tedious negotiations" had finally rid the city of the ex-superintendent. Day arrived from Boston on 1 May 1867, with five inebriates in tow from the Washingtonian Home. The south wing was now finished, and Day admitted 130 patients during his first year—about fifty more than Turner had treated throughout his three-year reign. Whereas no more than thirty-five patients had ever been present concurrently under Turner—and that number was rapidly dwindling by the end—Day stabilized the asylum's average population at fifty and then slowly increased it.[1] (But the asylum never came close to using its full capacity of three to four hundred beds.)

Dr. Albert Day: New Leadership and Philosophy

The treatment philosophy of Dr. Day was fully articulated in a treatise titled *Methomania,* published the same year as his arrival in Binghamton. Where Turner had emphasized control, Day emphasized instilling hope and self-confidence: "The patient must be first made to believe that his recovery will follow proper treatment. The idea has been so largely held . . . that recovery from this disease was impossible, . . . that the drunkard could not be reformed, . . . that those most likely to adopt this view . . . are the unfortunate victims of the disease themselves. . . . [I]t follows that the element of hope should be carefully nourished as a powerful stimulant to the other means employed." Day believed that the curability of inebriety should be instilled in the inebriate and that he should be taught that the source of that cure could be found within himself–that the price of liberty was eternal self-vigilance.[2]

The difference between the philosophies of Turner and Day was most evident in one policy: whereas most of Turner's patients had been legally committed and forced to stay against their will, all of Day's patients were voluntary. "This fact speaks volumes in favor of Dr. Day's system," the *Democrat* opined. What the volumes spoke was that the asylum was a going concern at last and that its governing philosophy had been set right: that is, brought into line with the thinking of Dr. Willard Parker and the board. The newspaper went on to explain the essence of Day's technique:

> Instead of locking intelligent men up behind bolts and bars, and treating them as criminals, insulting and degrading them as Mr. Turner did, Dr. Day from the first, endeavors to arouse in his patients the best feelings of their nature. He shows them that they yet have sufficient manhood and nobility to overcome a terrible evil. He for the first move, administers medicine of strengthening and soothing nature to the shattered frame, and when this is brought back to its natural state, he appeals to the best and truest feelings of the heart. He shows them the way in the path of honor, by placing confidence in them and treating them like men of honor, and there are very few indeed who abuse and violate this kindness. Some cases have indeed come to our knowledge, where confidence has been ungratefully met, but these are rare indeed.

In fact, the *Democrat* said, it would be difficult to find anywhere fifty "more highbred, cultivated, intelligent gentlemen than the present inmates," many of whom "hold exalted positions in life and society" and nearly all of whom are "actuated by the highest zeal and motives to reform." Over this noble community, truly "one large and happy family," Dr. Day spread the mantle of his paternal amiability.[3]

This was a higher class of patients than Turner had ever attracted, precisely the genteel clientele Parker had always desired; and they were now paying $10 to $20 a week for treatment, three months in advance. The president and board could not have been happier with the burgeoning prosperity of the institution and with Day's administration. As another newspaper remarked, the new superintendent "shows that no money is so well

invested as that which changes a live man from a social curse to a bless-
ing–giving him back to the state as a producer and not a mere consumer–
restoring him to his family and to the family of God."[4]

Albert Day, born in Wells, Maine, on 6 October 1812 (a decade before
Turner), had been cast upon his own resources at the age of thirteen by
the death of his father. He worked on a neighbor's farm, mastered a me-
chanical trade, married young, studied at night, and ultimately made his
way to Harvard Medical School. Like Turner's, Days' dedication to drunkards was inspired by the Washingtonian movement, in which he became
deeply involved. (The membership of the Washington Temperance Society had always included non-inebriates, who constituted a majority in
some chapters.) A total abstainer his entire life, Day entered Massachusetts politics not to advocate prohibition but rather to advance measures
in support of what became Boston's Washingtonian Home in 1857.[5] This
was truly "the first asylum that was opened for inebriates in the world."[6]

After becoming the first superintendent of the Washingtonian Home,
Day devoted nearly forty years to the asylum treatment of inebriates.
When his term in Binghamton ended in 1870, he opened a private asylum in Greenwood, Massachusetts, which burned down in 1873. He then
resumed his career as superintendent of the Washingtonian Home for
another twenty years, during which he was nationally recognized as a
spokesman for the medical approach to inebriety. Day retired just a year
before his death at eighty-one in 1894, at which date he was, according to
T. D. Crothers, "the oldest pioneer worker in this new field." He had dealt
with more inebriates–upward of 30,000–than anyone else.

In Crothers's opinion, Day's enduring success derived not only from his
perennial cheerfulness and compassion but also from his shrewd evasion
of the ideological and political strife that surrounded the treatment of inebriates during the nineteenth century. Never much of a medical scholar,
Day was the consummate practitioner, flexible and eclectic in his methods
and adroitly misleading in his public statements about them: "On the plat-
form as a public speaker, in his contact with patients, and everywhere, he
seemed to accept all the moral teachings of others, and added to them the
most pronounced materialistic rational means of treatment, which were
accepted without controversy." That is, Day tactfully and tactically steered
a middle course between the moral and medical models, mixing them
freely–and, to avoid contention, somewhat surreptitiously–despite their

apparent incompatibility. This mix was evident in Day's views toward the sources of inebriety (which he saw as both medical and characterological) and his view of those for whom he was caring. "Let it be remembered," he wrote in *Methomania*, "that such a man is diseased, and that he is fighting not against temptation only, but against temptation fostered and encouraged by the morbid elements of his own physical and mental nature."[7] Day employed a therapeutic bait-and-switch insofar as patients were drawn by a moral message into the asylums he ran and then treated more medically than they might have expected. "The appeals and prayers and pledges, and the physical means used continuously, were forces that sent many poor unfortunate inebriates back to health again," according to Crothers. But Day always gave priority to "the power of ideas, and the mental force of suggestion" to effect a cure.[8]

Crothers's view is corroborated by firsthand accounts of Day's new day at the New York State Inebriate Asylum, where he was soon beloved by the patients and the community alike. James Parton, in his 1868 *Atlantic Monthly* article, described Day's administration as "founded on the expectation that the patient and the institution will co-operate. If a man does not desire to be reclaimed, and such a desire cannot be awakened within him, the institution can do no more than keep him sober while he remains an inmate of it." The new superintendent's two "grand objects" were "to raise the tone of the bodily health, and to fortify the weakened will." Parton characterized Day as a type of the "good Yankee," temperamentally "accustomed to persuade and convince, not drive, not compel." The physician embraced his charges as if they were "younger brothers taken captive by a power stronger than themselves." His respect toward patients "must be balm to men accustomed to the averted look and taunting epithet, accustomed, too, to something far harder to bear,–distrust and abhorrence of themselves."[9]

To build trust, inmates were allowed, with the superintendent's counsel and consent, to visit Binghamton for outings and errands, and no one who actually sought Day's permission had yet "proved unequal to the temptation." A few others sneaked into town and got drunk, Parton admitted, but these were greeted upon their return with the mercy of a father for a prodigal son: "Lapses of this kind are not frequent, and they are regarded by the superintendent as part of the means of restoration which the institution affords; since they aid him in destroying a fatal self-confidence, and in inculcating the idea that a patient who lapses must never think of giving up the struggle, but renew it the instant he can gain the least foothold of self-control."

Some men, Day believed, "*must* fall, at least once, before the last rag of self-confidence is torn from them." Such falls were discouraged not by discipline and punishment but rather by the force of "Public Opinion" within the community of the asylum. A patient under Turner once had won the favor of his peers by smuggling a bottle into his room and inviting them to share it. Under Day, such an inmate would be widely shunned: "One of their number, suddenly overcome by temptation, who should return to the Asylum drunk, they would all receive as cordially as before; but they would regard with horror or contempt a man who should bring temptation into the building, and place it within reach of those who had fled hither to avoid it."[10]

This reliance on the power of group conscience resonates with the later practice of Alcoholics Anonymous toward "slippers." Many of Day's ideas, indeed, can easily be translated into AA discourse: his patients had to take the First Step, as it were: admitting that they were powerless over alcohol and that their lives had become unmanageable. Day's three cardinal rules foreshadowed AA principles that a drunk must "hit bottom" and ask for help before he can recover, that there is no excuse for a drink, and that recovery requires the alcoholic to change people, places, and things. As Day put it: "1. No hope for an inebriate until he thoroughly distrusts the strength of his own resolution; 2. No hope for an inebriate except in total abstinence as long as he lives, both in sickness and in health; 3. Little hope for an inebriate unless he avoids, on system and on principle, the occasions of temptation, the places where liquor is sold, and the persons who will urge it upon him."[11]

On their admission to the asylum, Day immediately removed patients from alcohol, not allowing them to taper off; and he warned them to beware of physicians who might prescribe a therapeutic glass of wine or, as was common in the period, "tinctures prepared with alcohol, which had often awakened the long-dormant appetite."[12] This, too, chimes with AA's traditional distrust of doctors because of their all too common naiveté about alcoholism.

Day also anticipated modern psychopharmacological theories in his attributing the inebriate's susceptibility to relapse to permanent changes in the brain (of course, he observed morphological rather than biochemical abnormalities). He once autopsied a reformed drunkard who had lived for some years as a teetotaler. "He found, to his surprise, that the globules of the brain had not shrunk to their natural size. They did not exhibit the inflammation of the drunkard's brain, but they were still enlarged, and seemed ready on the instant to absorb the fumes of alcohol, and resume their former condition." Such a man, Day hypothesized, was primed to revert to full-blown inebriety from a single drink: "He saw the citadel free from the enemy, swept and clean, but undefended, incapable of defense, and its doors opened wide to the enemy's return; so there was no safety, except in keeping the foe at a distance, away beyond the outermost wall."[15]

Asylum Life

In 1869 the *Atlantic Monthly* followed up Parton's piece with an insider's perspective. Published anonymously, this two-part article was written by John Willamson Palmer (1825–1906), a physician and occasional author of fiction, who had entered the asylum for treatment in 1868. Palmer described being awakened each morning by the sonorous ringing of a bell and looking about his snug but sufficiently spacious room. His extraordinarily detailed survey of its contents provides the best account we have found of the asylum's interior environment:

> Walls lofty and sky-colored; door and double window tall and dignified,–the latter provided with liberal panes and inside latticed shutters; wood-work of oak and dark cherry, handsomely molded and paneled; a portly oaken wardrobe, with double doors and drawers, and a certain imposing aspect, conveying the impression of "presence"; a hospitable carpet in warm colors; "all the modern improvements" for ablution, represented by a marble tank and silver-plated turn-cock; a double register for hot air and ventilation; pendent gas-fixtures, in good style, with globes and side-light; two tables, with cloth covers, in bright patterns of crimson and black, for periodicals, papers, and writing materials; a rather wide bedstead, of bronzed iron, in the English style, and on rollers; a lazy rocking-chair, and two office chairs in black walnut,–one with, the other without, arms; a looking-glass, not "palatial," but enough, and neatly framed; two wall brackets, at present surmounted by an opera-glass, three "blue-and-gold" volumes of verse, and a memory and a hope in the pictured loveliness of a girl; on the wall large photographs of Winterhalter's "Florinde," Rosa Bonheur's "Horse Fair," Mazerolle's "Anacreon," a Venus and Cupid, with doves, of Correggio; the

"Campanile at Florence" in water-colors, a rack full of *cartes de visite* and
steel vignettes, and the foot and ankle in plaster of Palmer's "White Captive," a gift from the sculptor.[14]

Palmer had transformed one side of his wardrobe into a bookcase, to hold
250 of his own volumes.[15] But aside from the sculpture and a few personal
touches, he wrote, his room was otherwise "in the uniform style of the
house."

This was the style chosen by Turner, and it reflected the conventions of
nineteenth-century asylum design in its attention to ease and tranquility
(for instance, in the selection of innocuously familiar art). Ironically, however, the soothing atmospherics were far better suited to Day's indulgent
practices than to Turner's Spartan ones. The cornerstone of Day's treatment, according to Palmer, was *confidence*, defined as "the largest liberty
reconcilable with the safety of the subject." If Day had been asked to define
his "system," the superintendent would have said: "To coax patiently into
life again the moribund conscience and will of each individual *protégé* and
ward of ours, and then endow him with power to complete his own cure,
by making him an eager, potent agent, with experience and opportunity,
in the cure of others. It is a system of a common motive, applied with
means in common, to the attainment of a common end."[16]

This statement, too, jibes with the "system" of Alcoholics Anonymous—
as does Palmer's tribute to the fellowship of the asylum's patients. In their
social intercourse, he wrote, the inmates constituted "a pure democracy,—
quintessential Americanism, asserting itself in that freedom of opinion to
which there is no limit but generosity, and of expression upon which no
restriction is imposed save by courtesy and decorum." One of their favorite
slogans was that "we are all 'tarred with the same stick,' and by that same
token we stick together. . . . Fair Play and Inebriates' Rights,—generosity in
judgment, and consideration for the claims of the flesh in its frailty,—these
are the law to our minds and the way to our hearts. Our diverse person-
alities are blended and welded by a common need and longing, and the
individual is lost in the partaken trouble. Unlike ship-board life, which
shamefully uncovers the naked selfishness of a man, bringing to the sur-
face all his abject Me-ness, this more humanizing experience, conceived
in helplessness and brought forth in longing, makes generosity a relief
and fellowship a comfort."[17]

There were cooperative patients and complainers, glad-handers and

The New York State Inebriate Asylum, interior views. From *Harper's Weekly*, 25 December 1869. Drawn by C. E. H. Bonwill.

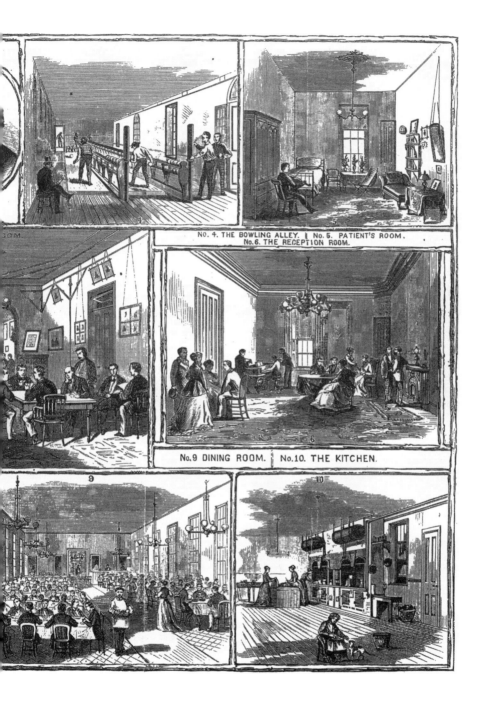

No. 4. THE BOWLING ALLEY. | No. 5. PATIENT'S ROOM.
No. 6. THE RECEPTION ROOM.

No. 9 DINING ROOM. | No. 10. THE KITCHEN.

isolators; all were tolerated except anyone perceived to be "self-seeking, sulky, captious, pharisaical, aloof from us, shy of us, ashamed of us, scornfully looking down from the cold heights of his moral 'green-seal' upon the cheap and humble contamination of our unaffected 'rot-gut,'–a snob among inebriates." For harmony's sake, such outside issues as politics and religious sectarianism were banned from general discussion. But gentle teasing flourished. "Here is a free school of manners, equal rights, and common sense, where are taught the fair play of the Golden Rule, and the decorous deference of the Hindoo Vedas."[18]

Although strict routines were few at the asylum under Day, the superintendent did institute a program of weekly evening activities–following the common meal, at which Day and his family were always in attendance: an egalitarian gesture much appreciated by the inmates. Mondays were set aside for meetings of the Literary Society, in the asylum chapel, at which lectures or literary readings were presented. Subjects covered during 1868 included "Columbus, a Study of Character"; "Oliver Goldsmith"; "Early English Novelist"; "The Passions, with Poetical Illustrations"; "The Telegraph, by an Operator"; "The Age, and the Men for the Age"; "Geology"; "Resources of Missouri"; and "The Inebriate Asylum, under the Regime of Coercion" (that is, the bad old days under Turner). An occasional visitor also participated. The most famous was Harriet Beecher Stowe, whose son Frederick was a patient.[19] Asked to read a passage from *Uncle Tom's Cabin,* she graciously agreed, using the only available copy, "a cheap double-columned pamphlet brought from the South by a freedman, now the porter of the Asylum."[20]

Thursday evenings were devoted to "dramatic receptions" to which the citizens of Binghamton were invited. In the compact but well-equipped theater, inmates taking both male and female parts staged amateur theatricals, sometimes with musical accompaniment. The fare often ran to farces, but serious plays, such as *Macbeth,* were occasionally mounted.

Wednesdays were reserved for a talk by the superintendent on some aspect of temperance. "Pithy performances these," Palmer observed, "neither scientific nor rhetorical, but of the very mother-soil of the subject, awfully sound, and to the point,–at times with a directness so drolly excruciating as to make the squirming hearer feel as though he were a full bottle of 'S.T-1860-X,' and the spiral horror of an analyzer's corkscrew, with its cold, critical intelligence, were slowly but surely grinding into his head."[21]

Parton, who attended at least one such session, recounted how Day opened the meeting with a prayer and some brief remarks and then invited patients "to illustrate the point from their own experience." The topic that evening, as so often was the case, arose from "an occurrence which had just taken place at the institution, and had been the leading topic of conversation all that day." A patient discharged just that morning, full of sober resolution, had been returned to the asylum, dead drunk, only twelve hours later, having relapsed during a railroad delay that stranded him at a station, with time on his hands and intoxicating notions buzzing through his mind:

> How perfect is my cure! I have not once *thought* of taking a drink. Not even when I saw men drinking at the bar did it cross my mind to follow their example. I have not the least desire for whiskey, and I have no doubt I could take that "one glass" which Dr. Day keeps talking about, without a wish for a second. In fact, no man is perfectly cured till he can do that. I have a great mind to put it to the test. It almost seems as if this opportunity of trying myself had been created on purpose. Here goes, then, for the last glass of whiskey I shall take as long as I live, and I take it purely as a scientific experiment."

The incident, wrote Parton, perfectly served Day's intention for these Wednesday meetings, "that every inmate of the Asylum shall become acquainted with the nature of alcohol, and with the precise effects of alcoholic drinks upon the human system. He means that they shall comprehend the absurdity of drinking as clearly as they know its ruinous consequences."[22]

Tuesday and Saturday evenings belonged to the Ollapod Club, a literary and social organization established by the inmates in November 1868. Activities included the reading of learned papers, playing table games, and hosting monthly receptions in which the public joined. Palmer reported that the members (sixty at that time) were elected but that "our terms as to qualification are studiously liberal," so as to exclude only those notorious for "vicious practices" or those whose "coarseness of manners and habits" made them socially intolerable. The Ollapods were thus the cream of the inmate population, the most accomplished professional men, whose elite status gave the club "the moral power of its own public opinion." This constraining influence was applied first to themselves: every Ollapod pledged allegiance to bylaws that forbade him "to offend or bring disrepute upon our fellowship by presenting himself at any time or place under the influence of liquor." Offenders were required to submit "a becoming apology" to be read before the club; "frank and genuine confession" was met in kind by "the cordial and sympathetic applause" with which it was invariably accepted.[23]

The Ollapods implemented Day's strategy of exerting control indirectly, mainly through peer pressure: "We find no method of discipline so wholesome and effectual as brief confinement, patient forbearance, and rational appeals to their reviving sense of honor." The asylum thus replaced Turner's deep distrust of his patients' motives with Day's "theory which claims for the inebriate a recoverable judgment, sensible affections, and moral responsibility; and which, refusing any longer to coerce him as a criminal or confine him as a lunatic, proposes by positive aid and comfort, and confiding appeals to his reason, his affections, and his aspirations, to restore him to himself, his family, and society."[24]

Day's Difficulties and Departure

Even though the asylum may have entered its Golden Age under Day, his tenure was less than utopian. As Turner gleefully noted in his *History:*

> During the first three years of Dr. Parker's scheme of trusting to the honor of the inebriate patients, there were three suicides among them; one homicidal case which ended in the stabbing of the superintendent, Dr. Day; four other deaths from alcoholism, besides many little irregularities among the patients, such as being arrested in town; fined and committed to jail for drunkenness and disturbing the peace; remaining overnight in town, and going back to the Asylum in the grey of the morning with their pockets loaded and themselves loaded,–the sympathizing friend in waiting to help them through the window and into bed. Such were frequent occurrences at the Asylum under Dr. Parker's administration. (*H,* 244 n)

Such "irregularities," of course, would never have been tolerated under the old order, during which, as Turner proudly stated, there had never been a fatality, much less an assault on the superintendent–the inevitable result, Turner thought, of relaxing discipline and putting inmates on their "honor."

Turner, in fact, had once visited the Home for the Fallen, the precursor of the Washingtonian Home in Boston, and he was decidedly unimpressed. "I was surprised," he wrote in an 1859 letter, "to find that it had no medical head for its management, no classification, no control, no definite treatment for its patients; in a word that it possessed not a single element required for the successful medical treatment and the radical cure of the inebriate." He seems not to have noticed that Dr. Day had already taken charge in Boston, but even if he had, he would have not have respected Day's approach.[25]

Ironically, the same was becoming true for the asylum trustees; by 1870, relations between Day and the board were evidently turning sour. In March the *Binghamton Democratic Leader* suggested that the trustees were now as eager to dispose of Day as they once had been to expel Turner. "That they are not in complete accord is well known. How can they be? Dr. Day is a man who never drank a glass of spirits in his life, and is known far and wide for his exertions in favor of total abstinence; while of the board of resident trustees [Parker, a temperance advocate, lived in New York], not a single man is any how prominently identified with the cause of temperance reform."

Day became convinced, Senta Rypins says, "that the other trustees were putty in the hands of [Ausburn] Birdsall, who had emerged as the strong man in the picture, if not the villain, and was shamelessly manipulating every situation to his own advantage."[26] According to the *Leader*, Birdsall charged Day "with a want of executive capacity." That capacity, in any event, had been narrowly delimited by interference from the board: "Nominally the superintendent, he is such only in name for they have deprived him of all executive authority. Dr. Day cannot even employ or discharge a kitchen scullion. That business must all be done by the trustees." More seriously, the board had usurped Day's right to determine who properly belonged in the asylum: "He came near losing his life by a reversal of his decision in a case of this kind last fall; when he was stabbed in an affray with a patient whom he had discharged as incurable, but who was readmitted by the trustees."[27]

As with Turner, a fire at the asylum provided a pretext to oust Day. According to Turner, the March 1870 blaze occurred "on the night of the day on which a bitter fight between Dr. Day, Superintendent, and Mr. Birdsall, Vice-President of the Asylum, ended in the defeat of Dr. Day and his friends." It is not clear what occasioned this particular quarrel, but it brought to a boil the simmering disputes over temperance politics and Day's administrative prerogatives. Immediately after the fire, Birdsall published a pamphlet accusing Day and his friends of torching the asylum. "This little episode," Turner observed, "gave Dr. Day an insight and a taste of Mr. Birdsall's venom, and his eyes were then opened to the position of the founder" (H, 271–72).[28] That there was arson is possible–it may have been the revenge of a disgruntled patient–but that Day was complicit is as incredible as the old charges against Turner.

Upon his arrival in 1867, Day had heard endlessly about his predecessor's alleged misdeeds. He had been told, writes Rypins, "how Turner had ruined the most promising venture of the century by his autocracy, behaving as if the asylum had been his private residence, inviting friends and relatives to live there as his guests, entertaining and lording it over all like a landed squire, using asylum labor to work his own farm nearby, and so on." But now he "said openly that he thought Turner must have been as much sinned against as sinning."[29]

Day read the handwriting on the wall and resigned his post on or about 10 May 1870. His disconsolate patients unanimously issued a testimonial implicitly absolving Day of responsibility for the rottenness of a few bad apples. The "system of moral restraint," they attested, "is the only true principle from which practical or permanent reformation can be either expected or hoped." The best evidence of its success was the rarity with which "the confidence of their Superintendent has been abused by the indulgence of his patients in strong drinks–a result which, it is our firm belief, could in no way have been attained by arbitrary treatment or physical restraint."[30] Turner, of course, would have begged to differ with this assessment.

Moral Reform versus Medical Treatment

The issue of physical restraint had been at the molten core of Turner's volcanic disputes with Parker and the board, as it was at the center of the wider cultural debate over the treatment of inebriates. At the opposite pole from Day's Washingtonian leniency stood those who advocated uncompromising severity. The tenets of this camp had been unequivocally stated by Andrew McFarland, superintendent of the Illinois State Hospital for the Insane, in a September 1866 letter to Turner. McFarland did not believe that inmates of inebriate asylums required any less restraint than those of insane asylums; in fact, they needed *more:* "I can trust to the honor of an insane man, be his disease acute or chronic, with far more assurance of safety than to that of the inebriate." The problem, he argued, was that a "false idea in regard to the inebriate has got possession of the public mind" as a consequence of "the multitude of Washingtonian lecturers—reformed drunkards—who perambulate the country, making themselves out something nobler than men who never wallowed in the gutter." The new common sense seemed to be "that these noble attributes only need to be unlocked from a temporary enthrallment by a sort of legerdemain—which nobody exactly defines—and that the noble instincts which have been held in abeyance will vindicate their natural supremacy over those 'unfortunate addictions' by which the subject has been made a victim. . . . They [the Washingtonians] seem to have been successful in throwing round a vice the mantle of a misfortune, and to have caused the public to look on an inebriate asylum as the place where salve is kept for such stricken natures."[31]

Explicit here is the clash between the moral and medical paradigms of habitual drunkenness that coexisted uneasily throughout the nineteenth century or were combined into an unstable compromise formation. The moral paradigm, dating from colonial times, held that because there was nothing inherent either to a person or to alcohol itself that prevented anyone from drinking moderately, it followed that individuals ultimately had control over and responsibility for their intake of alcohol. To drink excessively was a vice, and because to err was human, everyone had a more or less equal opportunity to become a drunkard. This moral view of *intemperance* as a sin was gradually overshadowed by the medical idea of *inebriety* as a disease of the mind and body characterized by an inability to curtail excessive drinking. The emergent medical paradigm was deeply influential within the temperance movement. It created a sympathetic attitude toward drunkards and gave rise to reformist attempts to save them from their powerlessness over alcohol, which was now thought by some physicians to be inevitably addicting.

Consider, for example, an 1858 letter to Turner from Edward C. Delavan, a prominent temperance reformer, on the occasion of laying the cornerstone for the New York State Inebriate Asylum. "I cannot but look upon this Institution," Delavan wrote, "as one of the happy results of the Temperance reform; when that reform commenced, the drunkard was generally looked upon with contempt, and an outcast, as a degraded being not worth an effort to save. . . . Now he is viewed by good men with compassion and love, as a brother to be saved, having a sore disease requiring the kindest attention, and the best medical skill and advice."[32]

As understood by physicians during the mid-nineteenth century, the concept of inebriety covered addiction both to alcohol and to other drugs, particularly opiates. *Alcoholism*, a term not coined until 1849 and not found in general circulation for a century after that, had more narrowly clinical connotations in Victorian usage than it later did; it referred not to habitual drunkenness but rather to the long-term physical consequences of alcohol addiction. In its broader modern sense, *alcoholism* is more or less synonymous with what the Victorians called *dipsomania*, a medical term that came into favor after the Civil War, gradually displacing *inebriety* and remaining in use (often shortened to *dipso*) until World War II.

In the holograph of Turner's annual report for 1866, for example, we find that the word *inebriety* has been systematically overwritten by Turner as *dipsomania*–as in the following key description:

> We define dipsomania as a disease, *sui generis*, produced by alcoholic poison–acute or chronic in its character, constitution and often hereditary– having an independent pathology and a morbid anatomy, which are as well marked as that of any other disease. It is found in *post mortems* of dipsomaniacs, by rummaging among the viscera and scrutinizing the organs and tissues of the body, that the brain, the stomach, the liver, the lungs, the heart, the kidneys, the intestines, *each* and *all*, present the ravages of alcoholic poison.[33]

The implications for treating dipsomania as a medicalized entity seemed clear enough. Valentine Mott, Turner's mentor, once used a memorable orthopedic metaphor. The disease of inebriety, he said, produced in its victim the equivalent of "a compound fracture from the crown of his head to the sole of his foot, as well as mental and moral dislocation." To treat such a malady with success, "the legal splint and bandage must be applied to hold this sick man in place during the process of healing, or the treatment fails, and the patient dies."[34]

If alcohol was a poison that denatured every organ of the human body and gravely affected mental operations, then the disease of inebriety, including its symptomatically destructive behaviors, should logically be attributed to the poison rather than to any innate depravity in the drinker.

As one medical authority put it, "The frenzy to destroy, or to quarrel, vex, torment, and cruelly maltreat inoffensive persons, and even the most affectionate friends and helpless children, is positively the result of alcoholic poisoning and irritation, and not a mark of transmitted sinfulness."[35] Such thinking was anathema, however, to the many religious leaders who regarded inebriety as a moral issue, as willful intemperance.

The philosophical issue was (and is) this: if drunkards have a disease, how can they be held accountable for its seemingly sinful side effects? In a strictly medical model they cannot. Yet moral and medical models not only collided during the nineteenth century; they also merged. The sin and disease paradigms, which seemed fundamentally irreconcilable on the matter of free will versus determinism, were nonetheless combined in ways that papered over the contradictions.

In his trenchant 1858 address during the dedication of the asylum, for example, Henry W. Bellows rejected the "bold and challenging line of division, where none has yet been made, between the *intemperate* and the *inebriate*–between *intemperance* as a moral, and *inebriety* as a corporal disease."[36] The truth, he insisted, was more complex:

> It may–it will be said, that intemperance is, in *all* cases, *partly* a habit and *partly* a disease–that, however originated, it tends in all cases to become a disease–and that physical and bodily diseases caused by voluntary excesses, must be cured by voluntary self-denials: that to allege that intemperance is a necessity of some bodily organizations–or that it is so often the result of automatic causes as to deserve and require to be taken out of the category of immoralities and placed among those of misfortunes–is to weaken the sense of personal responsibility in those liable to become its victims, and thus to take away what must ever be the grand check to its spread.

Granted even that a few cases of intemperance might be wholly moral or wholly corporal, still the rule of thumb should be "that, allowing it to more moral than corporal, in the majority of cases, it is more corporal than moral in the rest; and that, when and as long as the moral continues the exciting and perpetuating cause, it is to be treated morally; when and as long as the corporal continues the exciting and perpetuating cause, it is to be treated corporally."

As for "conceding that drunkenness often originates in necessary and self-acting causes"–that is, in determinants that would obviate individual moral responsibility – "there is not the least reason to fear, that to make provision for the rescue of the miserable victims of an hereditary or abnormal appetite for drink, will diminish in the least, in those conscious of the power and obligations of self-control, the disposition or the conscience to exercise them." Moral arguments, then, did not need be an impediment to medical treatment. The issue could be resolved by an appeal to pragmatic and Christian principles: "It is not necessary to prove that the subjects of this Institution [the inebriate asylum] are innocent and merely unfortunate persons, to justify, on moral grounds, its establishment. . . . Pity and protection, not only for the unfortunate, but also for the guilty, is the ever-growing policy, the ever-justified experience of modern philanthropy."

To finesse the conundrum of free will versus determinism, however, Bellows was forced to make one crucial concession with inescapably antidemocratic implications: namely, that with inebriates the will is unequally free:

> True, this doctrine does not claim that the will is perfectly free in each and every man – that the soul is, at the start, and in every case, superior to the body. But it does assert that, characteristically, by intention and by destiny, the will is free, and the soul eminent over the body, as over all things seen and tangible. It denies, it must be confessed, that modern doctrine of absolute and equal powers and capacities in all men – that irrational theory of individuality, which disintegrates the race into its component parts, and makes each atom of humanity complete in itself, the center of the universe, capable at once of all things which any other is capable of, independent of all others in its education and its fate. [Bellows may have been thinking here of Emersonian Transcendentalism.] Such a doctrine is as false to fact as it is arrogant, indocile, and unsocializing in its sentiment. There is no truth to history, to feeling, to Christianity, or to the staring [*sic*] modern experience, in it.

Bellows's address was an unusually lucid statement of the Victorian compromise formation that delicately mediated between the moral and medical models.[37] Here free will and determinism were placed on a continuum. Vice was seen to have led to physical corruption; possessed of free will at first, the drunkard incrementally lost it with every drink he took. Thus he was culpable of willfully tempting fate by picking up the bottle in the first place and thus putting himself at risk of contracting the disease of inebriety. The drunkard was understood to exhibit an innate weakness of will, which alcohol exploited. Inebriety was linked to intemperance, therefore, because self-poisoning was linked to attenuated will power. Alcohol addiction was not simply a physical disease but a disease of the will as well. Addiction was not located exclusively in the substance (alcohol as poison); it was inseparable from defective character, for the proper building of which Victorians held each other morally accountable. As Mott asserted along the same lines in 1861, "We wish to rescue the unfortunate victims of this disease from their constitutional malady, even though their condition may have been incurred by their own folly, and though they may have become so insane as to love the bondage."[38]

In a retrospective lecture in 1896, T. D. Crothers outlined this confluence of moral and medical models. He distinguished three types of opponents to the pure disease model to which he and Turner had subscribed. One group "flatly contradicted this theory, and asserted that all drinking was vice and moral disorder." A second group, composed of temperance societies and clergymen, also distrusted the disease model but not so much because it was false as because it might provide an excuse for (and hence a subtle incentive to) drinking and irresponsibility. In this view, the disease model could turn out to be just "another scheme of the rum power, to make inebriety respectable." The third group, which corresponds to what we have described as the Victorian compromise formation, consisted of reformers and religious philanthropists who "accepted the disease theory in part, especially in extreme degrees of alcoholic excess, but insisted that all cases were moral lapses at first. That first vice, then disease, existed, and the treatment must be directed to the vice side always."[39]

These groups had different approaches to the treatment as well as the causes of drinking problems. The first, the strictly moral group, believed that the transgressive impulse of intemperance could be blunted, if at all, only by punishment and suffering. The second, the more liberal group, relied on religious conversion to effect a saving change of heart. The third, with its notion of diseased will, saw a remedy in the pledge and in the mutual aid that characterized the Washingtonians. By contrast, adherents of the medical paradigm saw no value in moral suasion or religious conversion, although, ironically, they sometimes resembled the strict moralists in their stress on regulating what they called a disease rather than a vice. Turner exemplified how the seemingly compassionate disease model could coexist with a coercive method of treatment, with its premium on top-down control.

Understanding Turner's position involves one other contextual complication: the two Victorian categories of inebriates correlate not only with social class but also with the nature-versus-nurture binary that has shaped Western thought since the Renaissance. The idea of dipsomania as a congenital, "chemical" form of insanity was widely disseminated throughout the late nineteenth century, mainly through the mandatory drug education programs initiated in public schools by the Woman's Christian Temperance Union and other anti-drink organizations. A passage from an 1883 textbook designed for such classroom use epitomized the prevailing view: "Certain writers on diseases of the mind allude especially to a form of insanity called *dipsomania,* in which state a man has a maddening thirst for alcoholic drinks." Dipsomania denotes the extreme case of an "appetite for alcoholic liquors" that, according to "some of the best medical authorities," may be "inherited, just as people inherit such diseases as scrofula, gout, or consumption."[40] Within the social Darwinist framework of such textbooks, the inebriate (or dipsomaniac) was regarded as clinically insane, the defective offspring of degenerate stock. By definition, such a creature was radically different from a normal person.

Similar views still had currency early in the twentieth century. In one popular book about drinking, published in 1915, drunkards were said to fall into two types: "Now, of your two drunkards, one is morally defective from the start–a moral imbecile of a sort; that was the cause of his taking to drink. The other drunkard had to set up a pathological process which would bring him to the same state of moral imbecility. The one was born to his drunken inheritance, the other prepared himself for it. The one was diseased at the start; the other took his self-appointed way, through vice, to the identical degenerative condition of disease."[41]

In slightly different terms, the same distinction had been drawn by Turner ("hereditary" versus "constitutional" inebriates) and also by Palmer in his 1869 article for the *Atlantic Monthly.* Drunkards may be sorted, Palmer wrote, into two equally demoralized "communities,"

first, by those well-recognized phenomena which are, in some cases, the painful fate of inheritance, in others the pernicious fruit of circumstance,– in the one instance, a question of temperament, congenital taint, inoculation, propensity; in the other, of accident, adverse fortune, the conspiracy of temptation with opportunity, resulting in a dominant vicious self-indulgence, and that prolonged abuse which revenges itself in the establishment of organic disease,—the former appealing to the sympathy and the concern of the moralist and social reformer, the latter demanding the relief of Medicine or the restraints of Law. And of these two classes it is hard to decide which is the more numerous, since experience and philosophic observation are forced to conclude that the drunkard is quite as often "born" as "made"; "the child is father of the man" as commonly as the man is of the child; and on this point it may be affirmed, with more of dreadful certainty than figurative extravagance, that *many a baby is born drunk.*[42]

What is striking here is the affinity posited, on the one hand, between moralists and social reformers and, on the other, between medicine and the law. Palmer implied a division of therapeutic labor. Whereas "made" drunkards were capable of responding to the care of moralists and reformers, "born" drunkards should be placed in the hands of professional authorities, who would control them by legal or medical means.

The appropriate object of such control was the congenital dipsomaniac, whose chances of full recovery were deemed to be small but whose threat to society was deemed to be large. Also, inevitably, this hard core of "born" drunkards was associated with the lower social orders—or, in Bellows's terms, with the lower moral orders: those "moral imbeciles" thought to be less innately capable of exercising free will. At the New York State Inebriate Asylum, as Palmer remarked, there was an "incorrigible minority" of inmates: "the puerile, and the stupid, who remain deaf to the voice of warning, and defiant of the claims of affection,—the unstable and the stolid, who are yet to be 'dead-beat,' these are they whom the Asylum merely *harbors.*" Such inmates might better have been put in a "House of Detention," for that was, to all intents and purposes, what the asylum had to become in order to accommodate them.[43]

For its more respectable clientele, however, especially those whose addiction was circumstantial and acquired, the asylum was truly a "House of Refuge," offering, Palmer said, "the freedom of a superior country hotel" in which "we are fortunate in being able to meet on an equal footing of confidence and respectful consideration." In short, the asylum became a kind of gentleman's club, which "'reforms' a man by helping him to reform himself":

It presupposes in him a sincere longing and an earnest effort, and it offers him wise moral conditions of patience, encouragement with kindly admonition, trust with well-timed warning, refuge from care and from temptation, cheerful and sympathetic companionship, improving and diverting mental exercise, and all the devices of sagacity and tact which his temper or his trouble demand; sound physical conditions, also, of rest (for there's no such tired wretch as your worn-out inebriate), regularity of habit, wholesome and substantial diet, pure air, free motion, animating games, hearty songs, and jolly laughter. And that is all—that is not humbug.[44]

Palmer was, of course, describing the post-Turner era at the asylum, the governing philosophy of which had shifted under Day's leadership from a militantly medical ethos toward the values we have described as moral, or else a moral accommodation of the medical. Day emphasized the drunkard's capacity, under nurturing conditions, to reform his will and therefore to regain his mental and physical health. Where the Turner regime was rigid and authoritarian, the Day system was lenient and egalitarian.[45]

The latter stemmed from the Washingtonian tradition of treating the drunkard, in Delavan's words, "as a brother to be saved, having a sore disease requiring the kindest attention and the best medical skill and advice." But the inmates most susceptible to such treatment corresponded to Palmer's gentlemanly first type—the sort Governor Lucius Robinson had in mind in 1879, when he shut down the New York State Inebriate Asylum as a "complete failure" because it was, he said, "practically nothing more than a hotel for the entertainment of wealthy inebriates."[46]

The Turner plan had been designed, on the contrary, for the type of inebriates Palmer would have consigned to prison or the insane asylum. By Palmer's lights, Turner's error had been to admit no practical distinction—and, implicitly, no class distinction—between "made" and "born" drunkards and to gear treatment exclusively to the latter. According to Crothers, Turner's ideal was "practically a workhouse hospital on a military basis, restraint and control being the cornerstone. Each case was regarded as a suicidal mania needing positive restraint and constant care and watching" (*S*, 311–12).

The logic of Turner's approach led to the model of involuntary confinement that Crothers advocated in an 1891 article titled "Are Inebriates Curable?" Yes, said Crothers, but only if the state is willing to get tough

with drunkards and design asylums accordingly—asylums that would be
far closer to Houses of Detention than to Houses of Refuge:

> These scientific ways of curing drunkards may be summarized as follows:
> First, legislate for their legal control, then organize industrial hospitals in
> the vicinity of all large towns and cities. Tax the spirit traffic to build and
> maintain such places, just as all corporations are made responsible for
> all the accidents and evils which grow out of them. Arrest and commit all
> drunkards to such hospitals for an indefinite time, depending on the re-
> storation of the patients; also commit all persons who use spirits to excess
> and imperil their own and the lives of others. Put them under exact mili-
> tary, medical, and hygienic care, where all the conditions and circum-
> stances of life and living can be regulated and controlled. Make them self-
> supporting as far as it is possible, and let this treatment be continued for
> years if necessary. The recent cases will become cured and the incurable
> will be protected from themselves and others, and made both useful and
> self-supporting.[47]

The icy severity of this proposal—its tone leeched of the overtly moral-
ized sentiment of Victorian religion but suffused with the covertly mor-
alized swagger of modern science—lays bare the latent repressiveness of
the emergent medical paradigm. Insofar as the treatment of inebriety was
to be scientific, it was also to be administered by a clinical hegemony. It
assumed, moreover, that because inebriety was a disease over which a
drunkard was powerless, he was incapable of free will; he had, in fact, sur-
rendered his will and thereby lost all claim to moral or physical autonomy.
Such drunkards had rendered themselves wards of the state, whose agents
seemingly had no choice but to deal with them custodially. This was the
view that won out when the New York State Inebriate Asylum was closed
as such and later reopened as an insane asylum that incidentally treated
incurable drunkards, then regarded as incapable of reformation except by
means of incarceration.

The Asylum's Decline

The entire asylum movement drifted toward the same end during the late
nineteenth century. The fine ideals that had established the humanitarian
institutions for "moral treatment" had given way to potentially inhumane
practices based on the hard-boiled realities of managing large and often

unruly inmate populations. Although little is know about the later years of the New York State Inebriate Asylum (1870–79), it is likely that this institution, too, gradually succumbed to custodial incarceration–at least for the indigent inmates involuntarily committed by judges across the State.[48] In an 1877 article, Dr. Daniel G. Dodge, the successor to Day as superintendent, noted that of 713 patients admitted between 1870 and 1872, 402 suffered from the "hereditary taint" of inebriety. It was some of the patients in this group, no doubt, to whom Dodge referred as those "depraved in all their instincts": hopeless cases who ought to be expelled, or at least separated from the more temperate inmates, preferably in a different sort of institution. Dodge went on to advocate legislation that pointed toward custodial incarceration: a law that would "give the superintendent the proper power to restrain, discipline, or even discriminately punish, mainly by closer detention, all refractory patients, whether voluntary or otherwise."[49]

It was apparently different, however, for the undepraved inmates, especially the paying customers. Over time, the asylum's superintendents became not only minions of the trustees but also–in a grotesque inversion of the Turner regime–wards of their wealthy residents. The annual report for 1877 suggested that the private patients, rather than their keepers, were setting the terms and conditions of their "confinement": "The Managers are of the united opinion that, whilst voluntary submission to treatment in the Asylum is capable of yielding the most gratifying results, it is at the same time subject to check and hindrance because of brief duration, the restlessness of the patient under restraint, and his over confidence in his ability to resist temptation upon again entering society, coupled with the consciousness that he is at liberty at any time to leave the institution."[50]

Moreover, the asylum population seems to have steadily decreased. In 1871, the first year after Day's resignation, 315 inmates were treated; 249 patients were admitted in 1876; only 164 in 1877; and by the end in 1879 only seventeen remained (about the same number as during Turner's last months)–and all but five or six of these were private patients, none of whom had recently arrived. One newspaper cynically noted that living at the inebriate asylum did not impede the "rich bummers" from "procuring all the liquor they desire, and every few days the inmates are found on our streets in a beastly state of intoxication." This same paper seconded the

Advertisement for the New York State Inebriate Asylum. From *Quarterly Journal of Inebriety* 1 (March 1877).

opinion of the *Syracuse Standard* that the asylum was "not only a failure, but a stupendous swindle."

It appears that the political infighting of the 1860s had ushered in a decade of outright corruption. The board came more and more to regard the asylum as a plum to be plucked for personal enrichment and political patronage. The sequence of superintendents after Day is not entirely clear, but at least the following men served: Dr. Daniel G. Dodge, from July 1870 through June 1873; Dr. Lyman Congdon, appointed in July 1873; Dodge again, from 1875 to March 1877; Dr. Daniel H. Kitchen, former chief of staff at the Charity Hospital on Blackwell's Island in New York, from 1877 to September 1878; Dr. Moreau Morris, former superintendent of the Metropolitan Health Board, from 1878 to 1879.[51] The frequent turnover may suggest something about the rigors of the job, but it more likely reflected the desire of the board and local politicians to have a pliant administrator in place. The asylum's officers, it was alleged by one newspaper report, "have been forced on it because they have rendered political service, not because they possessed medical skill or philanthropic earnestness."

By the late 1870s, rumors of rampant graft and mismanagement were widespread. Turner, for one, was convinced that Parker and his cronies—including "Boss" Tweed—had been skimming the asylum's income. Judge Charles H. Doolittle, a former trustee who had resigned in protest over Turner's ouster, wisecracked that the asylum's funds in the hands of Parker and his ilk "were about as safe against fraud, misappropriation and waste, as a National bank and its funds would be in the custody of a board of directors composed of professional thieves and burglars."[52]

Turner committed his suspicions to writing, first as part of his 1876 lawsuit against the trustees, and later in a memorandum too incendiary for general circulation.[53] The board under Parker, he alleged there, had encouraged "reckless extravagance" and lost sight of the patients in a scramble to "to make the asylum a popular resort." When the legislature finally looked into the asylum's "astonishing expenditures," the chairman of the investigating committee, a physician, was muzzled by being appointed superintendent; his negative report was buried. Two years later, this man (Dodge?) resigned, "having amassed a fine property"; his replacement was the "impecunious medical friend" (Congdon?) of an "honorable senator," whose appointment "strangled in its infancy" yet another state inquiry. Two years later, the former superintendent (Dodge again?) was reinstated "to further enrich himself and friends." About the same time, the board began to keep two sets of books so as to loot the asylum more efficiently.

With the retirement of the "astute superintendent" after another two years, Turner's memorandum continued, the "Utica Asylum ring" saw an opportunity to supplement its rake-off from that institution by converting the inebriate asylum into another state insane asylum. They installed their own favorite son (Kitchen?) at Binghamton, a man somewhat disadvantaged by the fact that he "had been turned out of one hospital for drunkenness and now after a year he was notoriously worse as an inebriate, than the patients he was supposed to cure." When he too was deposed, the "ring" began to lobby more insistently for the conversion of the asylum. But its friends "rallied once more" and put in place an honest superintendent (Morris?), who began "to build on the ruins of his predecessors." This did not sit well with the swindling politicians, who finally convinced the governor to pronounce the asylum an irredeemable failure.

> During this time over four hundred thousand dollars were received from patients, the records of which are either lost or destroyed; also three hundred and eighty thousand from the State and counties, which was supposed to be expended on the building, very little trace of which can be found; making in all nearly eight hundred thousand dollars, received and expended in this asylum, from *1866 to 1879;* an average of over sixty-one thousand dollars a year. As an instance of the interest manifested by the board of trustees, the reports show that fifty-eight thousand dollars were paid this board for professional services and traveling expenses, and that they contributed only one hundred and twenty dollars to help on the work.

Turner's indictment, of course, put the worst possible construction on the asylum's history. That it contained at least a germ of truth is suggested by press reports of incessant chicanery. The last board of trustees, said one such story, was "accustomed to squander other people's money in wasteful expense until their transactions had gone so far that in order to save themselves from exposure they transferred the property of a private corporation to the State for the nominal sum of one dollar." As suggested in chapter 2, the 1879 sale of the asylum to the state was probably illegal and possibly unconstitutional to boot. But Turner and his allies, already defeated in court, were helpless to reverse a fait accompli for which public support had been aroused by all the negative publicity. Bellows wrote the New York State Inebriate Asylum's epitaph: "I have survived them all [the original trustees], and I have seen the institution which they all loved so much and served so well, captured, plundered, sold and destroyed by their successors."[54]

The corruption apparently reached into the renewed construction at Binghamton, designed to enlarge the building to accommodate 1,600 insane inmates. More charges were brought; more investigations were made; several members of the reconstituted board were forced to resign in disgrace. But in the end the New York State Inebriate Asylum was officially dissolved on 1 June 1879. It reopened two years later as the Binghamton Asylum for the Chronic Insane, and under different names, it stayed in operation for a century.

At the dedication of the inebriate asylum in 1858, Valentine Mott had prophesied of Turner: "His name will shine forth as one of the most distinguished among the great and good men, not only of our own country, but of the whole civilized world, and in all coming time."[55] The building, now stripped of its former magnificence, still occupies a hillside east of Binghamton, dimly visible from cars shooting past on the interstate: a vacant and ruined monument to its forgotten founder's blasted dreams.

5

Lessons and Legacies

Drunkard's Refuge tells a story and sheds light on a particular cultural context within which that story unfolded. The story is about a man, Dr. J. Edward Turner, and an institution, the New York State Inebriate Asylum. The context is the historical emergence of addiction mutual aid societies and professionally directed treatment institutions in America and the larger reform movements of which they were a part. Whereas the story is confined to a particular time and place, the context predated and extended long beyond the passing of Turner and his asylum. This last chapter explores the fate of the larger field in which the New York State Inebriate Asylum played such a historical role and offers some reflections on what meaning we have extracted from our study of its story.

The Fall of Nineteenth-Century Addiction Treatment

In the 1890s the future of addiction treatment in America looked bright to the leaders of the nation's first treatment institutions. In 1891, Dr. T. D. Crothers, the field's most prolific writer and one of its most visible spokesmen, characterized its future as "promising" and predicted that "the public will support inebriate asylums with increasing generosity."[1] Crothers remained optimistic throughout the decade, proclaiming in the pages of the *Journal of Inebriety* in 1899 that "no other journal has ever lived to see the principles and truths it attempted to promulgate so fully accepted and endorsed" and that the "light of the new century coming up the dawn is already radiant with promises of greater progress."[2]

Progress *had* been made in medicalizing and destigmatizing addiction to alcohol and other drugs. The treatment and reformation of inebriates was emerging as a specialty within the professional fields of medicine and religion. The number of institutions specializing in addiction treatment had increased from six in 1870 to several hundred by the mid-1890s. Proprietary franchises and home cures too were enjoying explosive growth (and profit). Some state legislatures were providing financial support for inebriate asylums and passing involuntary commitment laws to force inebriates into institutional care, while hundreds of thousands of citizens were voluntarily seeking the assistance of these facilities. The leaders of the inebriate homes and asylums had been brought into professional association; not only did their ideas fill issue after issue of the *Journal of Inebriety,* but there was also a virtual explosion of professional books bearing such titles as *Diseases of Inebriety; The Psychology of Intemperance; Inebriety: Its Causes, Its Results, Its Remedy; The Opium Habit and Alcoholism;* and *Alcohol Inebriety: From a Medical Standpoint.* Yet despite these achievements and the predictions of a great future, addiction treatment as a professionally directed specialty had virtually disappeared by the early 1920s—a turn of events foreshadowed by the fall of the New York State Inebriate Asylum. Only a few nineteenth-century addiction treatment programs survived into the second half of the twentieth century, and none from that period exists today.

Many factors led to that collapse, among them the unanticipated economic panics that eroded financial support for these enterprises. Most of the nineteenth- and early twentieth-century inebriate asylums and inebriate homes had been funded by a combination of public monies (including some direct allocation of alcohol tax revenues), private philanthropy, and patient fees. Many institutions closed during periods of economic hardship as public funds were reallocated to other areas, philanthropic donations decreased, and the admission of self-paying patients declined.

More important was an ideological shift within American culture away from the view that alcoholism was a treatable disease. As the nineteenth century closed, the nation moved toward a reactionary redefinition of its alcohol-related problems. In this view, which resembled that of gospel temperance, the problem lay not in the unique vulnerability of a minority of alcohol and drug consumers but in the products themselves and in the vice-filled institutions, the saloon and illicit drug traffic, that were aggressively promoting them. Those addicted to alcohol came to be redefined as depraved rather than diseased. The solution seemed clear: let the existing drunkards die off, and prevent the creation of new drunkards through the vehicles of temperance education, the total abstinence pledge, and the legal prohibition of the sale of alcohol. The shift from a medical to a moral/criminal model of alcoholism undermined the legitimacy and future of treatment efforts.

This shift reached its climax with the ratification in 1919 of the Eighteenth Amendment to the Constitution, which launched America's "noble experiment" with alcohol prohibition. Perhaps one of the best-kept secrets in American history is just how well Prohibition worked *at first.* Inebriate homes, asylums, and proprietary institutes closed in droves as alcohol-related problems and patient admissions plummeted during the early 1920s.[3] (Not until the late 1920s were most alcohol-related problems again on the rise.)

The weakened field of addiction treatment found itself unable to repel economic and political threats. Several factors contributed to the field's professional and political impotence. Its public reputation had been wounded by highly publicized breaches of ethical conduct. Newspaper exposés charged incompetence and even fraud in clinical and business practices. Allegations abounded of medical malpractice, inadequate care, abuse of patients, dishonest marketing practices, excessive lengths of stay, and financial exploitation of patients and families. The repeated charges of chicanery and crime that pervaded the history of the New York State Inebriate Asylum were not unique. The heads of the proprietary addiction cure institutes were likewise bitterly attacked as financially motivated quacks.[4] Muckraking investigations of the bottled addiction "cures" exposed products secretly loaded with alcohol, opium, morphine, and cocaine. Such publicity unalterably damaged the reputation of nineteenth-century treatment institutions and diminished public support for their continued existence.

Because those institutions had catered mostly to an affluent population, they had done little to ease the burden that indigent alcoholics were placing on jails and community hospitals. Many facilities were viewed not as establishments that served their communities but rather as places for the rich to dry out and to escape the consequences of drunken misbehavior. As a result, few community leaders came to their defense when inebriate institutions faced extinction.

There were also problems of scientific credibility that grew out of the field's modality bias (sustained institutional sequestration), its poorly developed clinical technology (the subject of periodic newspaper exposés), and its aversion to the use of scientific methods to study addiction and evaluate treatment methods. Conflict within and between treatment institutions and between the addiction specialists and allied professions (particularly the emerging field of psychiatry) created a fragmented field that never was able to speak with one voice. And a failure to address problems of succession had over the years left the field without competent and energetic leadership to respond to emerging threats.

Nineteenth-century treatment institutions, then, faded from existence during the opening decades of the twentieth century, its leaders deceased or too demoralized even to record the field's demise. The last issue of the *Journal of Inebriety* was published in 1914, and the American Association for the Cure of Inebriety (renamed the American Society for the Study of Alcohol and Other Narcotics in 1904) collapsed in the early 1920s. As treatment centers closed, alcoholics were sentenced to jails ("drunk tanks," or "inebriate colonies"); some were repeatedly admitted for detoxification to the "foul wards" of city hospitals; others were housed on the back wards of state insane asylums; those with financial resources were recruited into a new generation of private "drying out" sanatoria and hospitals. It would take more than half a century to recreate the professional field of alcoholism treatment, and few of the pioneers within that reemerging field possessed any awareness of an earlier era when alcoholism treatment institutions dotted the American landscape.

It is also noteworthy that the collapse of nineteenth-century treatment institutions coincided with the dissipation of nineteenth-century mutual aid societies. Those seeking to evaluate the health and future viability of twenty-first-century addiction treatment institutions would be well advised to scrutinize the mutual aid societies from which many have drawn their sustenance and the role that such societies have played in spurring innovations in the professional treatment of alcoholism. One of the most fascinating dimensions of the history of addiction mutual aid and treatment in the United States is the unrelenting pervasiveness of its cycles of despair and hope. The spirit of the Washingtonian movement that inspired Drs. Turner and Day to devote their lives to the care of inebriates took new form after the collapse of most Washingtonian societies in the 1840s. Native American recovery circles, fraternal temperance societies, reform clubs, workplace recovery groups (the Dashaways), institution-based support groups (the Godwin Association, the Keeley Leagues), faith-based recovery groups (the Drunkard's Club, the United Order of Ex-Boozers, and the Jacoby Club) are all links in the historical chain leading from the Washingtonians to Alcoholics Anonymous and other contemporary recovery mutual aid groups.[5] Just as the Washingtonians' optimism and energy provided impetus for the rise of inebriate homes and asylums, Alcoholics Anonymous a century later reinstilled the cultural belief in the potential for recovery that would foster a new generation of treatment institutions.[6]

The Nature of the Addict and the Methods of Reform

The conflicts between Dr. J. Edward Turner and Dr. Willard Parker, as well as the differences between Drs. Turner and Day, represent two enduring and competing views about the nature of treatment and recovery. The regimes of Turner and Day, which mark the two major epochs in the brief history of the New York State Inebriate Asylum, not only reflected the divergent philosophies of inebriate asylums and inebriate homes but also set the themes for a debate that still continues.

The fundamental point at issue between Turner and Day was whether the inebriate was at his core Dr. Jekyll or Mr. Hyde. Although both men considered inebriety a disease, they viewed their patients quite differently. Turner saw the inebriate as Mr. Hyde: a liar, thief, homicidal/suicidal rogue who required legal restraint and physical sequestration until his morbid character could be modified. Turner even proposed lifelong involuntary confinement for inebriates of unmalleable character. Day, on the other hand, regarded the inebriate as Dr. Jekyll: a fundamentally honorable gentlemen whose best graces had been degraded by a poisonous chemical agent. Whereas Turner's approach was to suppress the diseased character of Mr. Hyde, Day's approach was to elicit the hidden integrity of Dr. Jekyll and to enlist his moral decency in resisting future exposure to alcohol. It was out of this basic difference that emerged very dissimilar treatment philosophies: one reliant on control, the other on care and trust; one emphasizing coercion, the other moral uplift; one based on a hierarchical model of expert medical treatment, the other on a partnership model that fortified the inebriates' will, ennobled their character, and then challenged them to carry a message of hope to other inebriates.

The tension between Turner and Day carried over into a disagreement regarding the role of community in the recovery process. For Turner, the family and community represented sabotage and temptation from which the inebriate had to be quarantined. For Day, however, the family and community were valuable resources for the mastery of temptations within the context of treatment. There is a similar dichotomy in current debates about the best approach to addiction treatment, the ideal length of treatment experience, the role of coercion in recovery, and the degree to which addicts seeking recovery need to be isolated from or reconnected to their families and communities.

Given the turbulent history and untimely demise of the New York State Inebriate Asylum and Turner's fall from grace within the very field he had created, it is easy to lose sight of the monumental achievement that is reflected in the opening of America's first medically directed treatment institution. How did Turner manage to develop a climate of acceptance for the inebriate asylum concept and generate financial support for it?

Extending the work of Benjamin Rush, J. E. Todd, and Samuel Woodward, Turner promoted a seminal idea and a new language that forced communities to redefine their perception of drunkenness and the drunkard. By helping to bring the medical language of inebriety and dipsomania into common usage and by disseminating the disease concept of these conditions, he challenged the nation to create a new kind of institution that could restore many inebriates to full citizenship. He used both his status as a physician and his personal charisma to carry this message.

Turner placed his proposal within the broader reform spirit of his time. A moral entrepreneur in the classic sense, he emulated the methods of other reformers, such as Dorothea Dix, by calling upon all Americans to be their brothers' keepers. More specifically, he argued that the drunkard was physically sick, could be helped, and was worthy of help—arguments that would be resurrected by Dwight Anderson and Marty Mann in the 1940s as the centerpiece of the modern alcoholism movement.[7] Turner's arguments tapped into a reform spirit in America that used new social institutions and new professions to help move the country closer to its utopian vision of a model society.

Such efforts have never been easy. Anyone today who has worked to organize prevention and treatment services has likely experienced the same kind of community resistance that Turner encountered in the mid-nineteenth century. His difficulties getting enabling legislation, raising funds to build the inebriate asylum, recruiting a board, and even assembling a quorum for early board meetings have all been recapitulated in many American communities in the intervening years. What this reveals is that social change involves developmental stages in a community's (or culture's) perception of a problem, in sentiments toward potential solutions to that problem, and in readiness to take action on a given strategy to resolve that problem. Tactics for social change must be carefully designed to match these stages.

Turner implicitly understood that significant social change comes through eliciting changes within major social institutions. He waged a relentless campaign of education and influence through prolific correspondence and face-to-face meetings. The targets of these communications were government (particularly state legislatures), medicine, religion, business, and the press. By working through these institutions, Turner laid the groundwork for the eventual support of his experiment in the medical treatment of inebriety. A century later a movement led by the National Committee for Education on Alcoholism, the Research Council on Problems of Alcohol, and the Yale Center of Alcohol Studies targeted these same institutions to lay the foundation of the modern field of alcoholism treatment.

The flaw in Turner's strategy was that the campaign petered out as the demands of building and operating the asylum consumed more and more of his time. What he failed to recognize was that the support that had created his asylum would be desperately needed to sustain the experiment. It became impossible simultaneously to manage the internal organizational environment and the outside political and social environment. One could build a case that the same thing happened following the success of the modern alcoholism movement: as grassroots alcoholism councils acquired financial resources and evolved into formal treatment agencies, their roles of community education and policy advocacy were abandoned to the day-to-day demands of operating prevention and treatment agencies.

Turner also proposed a key idea that exerted great influence on the funding of inebriate homes and asylums and has since been periodically revived: that every industry ought to be responsible for the injuries that grow out of it. Turner argued that inebriety was an inevitable byproduct of the alcohol industry and that either the industry or the government, which profited from alcohol taxation, should be liable for financing the treatment of unfortunate consumers. This argument was subsequently used to garner a portion of liquor license revenues in the 1860s to support such institutions as the Chicago Washingtonian Home and was revived as an argument undergirding the modern funding of alcoholism treatment.

The Rise and Fall of Social Reformers and Reform Institutions

What kind of man would be so compelled to take on a controversial cause that he would give up a career in mainstream medicine to devote himself to the care of stigmatized inebriates? It is common for such pioneers to be "wounded healers," individuals who have themselves escaped the devastation of inebriety or who have helplessly witnessed others succumb to it. The very characterological attributes that so often accompany the birth of reform movements—unswerving commitment, unchallengeable belief, unwavering tenacity, and boundless energy—can also be the seeds for the eventual fall of reform leaders and their institutions. The charisma of men like Turner is a double-edged sword: even as it opens a pathway for social change, it threatens to injure those who wield it. Thus, the very qualities that had enabled Turner to achieve his dream of opening an inebriate asylum became liabilities in his management of the institution. Constant encounters with what a social stigma evokes—indifference, discomfort, prejudice, and hostility—may magnify the characterological excesses of reformers into fatal flaws, particularly when these leaders, like Turner, seem to be operating without the buffer of strong professional and social support.

Some charismatic leaders such as Turner seem most vulnerable not in the drive for achieving their vision but when that vision is closest to fruition. This suggests that the temperament and skills required to launch social movements are very different from those required to maintain the institutions that are the fruit of such movements. Turner had no peer in the time and effort he invested in pioneering the first medically directed inebriate asylum in America, but he was ill suited to manage the complex professional and political relationships required to sustain the institution he had dedicated his life to creating.

That exact scenario has been replicated many times in the transition from a social movement to create alcoholism treatment programs to the actual organization and operation of such programs. In the mid-twentieth century, men and women cut from the same tree as Turner spent years laying the groundwork for community-based alcoholism and addiction treatment programs. Like Turner, many of those who successfully led these campaigns did not fare well as administrators, often experiencing similar conflicts with boards, staff, and clients. Some also suffered falls from grace due to perceived breaches in ethical or legal conduct. This vulnerability of social reformers might aptly be christened the Curse of Icarus: like their mythical counterpart, many addiction treatment pioneers have been burned when, in a state of self-intoxication, they flew too close to the sun. A lesson from the life of J. Edward Turner is that charismatic leadership (and the characterological flaws that often accompany it) must be consciously and actively managed at both personal and organizational levels.

How does one explain the toxic conflict that plagued so noble an experiment as the New York State Inebriate Asylum? How could dedicated professionals end up charged with incompetence, crime, and corruption? Had such issues been unique to Binghamton, New York, in the 1860s and 1870s, they would not warrant wide interest among modern readers. But destructive internal and external conflicts and charges of ethical and legal misconduct were not unique to America's first medically directed addiction treatment institution. Acrimony between executives and boards of treatment agencies (particularly board infringement into daily operations), public scandals, and zealous debates over conflicting treatment philosophies have been more the norm than the exception in the history of addiction treatment institutions. So how is the pervasiveness of such a phenomenon to be understood? We suggest three hypotheses.

First, as suggested above, there are certain characteristics common to leaders who champion care of the inebriate at times when the inebriate is generally viewed with contempt and hostility. To sustain such a cause requires characterological excesses that are likely to elicit hostility and engender conflict over time. We suspect that the lines separating faith and intolerance, vision and grandiosity, confidence and arrogance can be thin ones under such conditions. Turner's history underscores the point that the high level of passion required to found a treatment institution does not always translate into the business and clinical acumen requisite to manage it.

Second, perhaps there is also a propensity for organizations created to serve stigmatized populations to become more and more isolated—to evolve, as one of us has suggested elsewhere, into "closed incestuous systems."[8] As a result of sustained closure, some organizations implode in a wave of personality conflicts, ideological schisms, internal conspiracies, and the scapegoating of key individuals or organizational units. Turner could serve as the prototype of the "high priest" of such a system, and the relationship between Turner and Parker illustrates how conflicts between divergent philosophies of treatment and institutional management can crystallize within an increasingly polarized relationship between an executive and a board president. The history of the New York State Inebriate Asylum vividly demonstrates how such polarization can tear an organization apart and set it on a course of self-destruction.

A third hypothesis involves the stewardship of institutional resources. We have long witnessed the evolution of social movements into formal service organizations and then into businesses. It is in the latter two stages that resources once devoted to a service mission can get reallocated to other institutional or personal agendas. The progression was clearly illustrated during Turner's tenure in his preoccupation with the ornateness and beauty of his facility and its furnishing, compared with the energy he extended to those being cared for in that facility. It was also the case in the later days of the asylum when board members plundered the institution for their personal gain. This is to suggest not some unique moral failure of Turner and the board (although the board's actions were egregious) but rather the process of moral drift that is possible in all service organizations and the unrelenting scrutiny and care necessary in the stewardship of resources. The New York State Inebriate Asylum was not the last addiction treatment agency that lost its soul, its service mission, long before it closed its doors.

Turner's Place in the History of Addiction Treatment

We started this investigation unsure of how we would finally view Joseph Edward Turner as a physician and as a man. After sifting the available evidence, we do not believe that Turner was an arsonist or a thief; we do not see him as a criminal or a charlatan. But we also are sure that we would not want to have worked with him or for him in this venture. If Turner brought fatal flaws to the New York State Inebriate Asylum, they were flaws not in his vision but in his derisive attitudes and prickly personality. When two such powerful people collide—and we suspect that Turner and Parker were temperamentally akin—the result is often destructive, no matter how noble the vision that brought them together.

Turner comes across in our research as a nearly tragic figure who, from being the celebrated founder of a new social institution, became a public and professional pariah never able to rehabilitate his own reputation. He never attended, let alone enjoyed prominence within, the American Association for the Cure of Inebriety—the association that represented the field he could well be said to have created; he was never accorded the distinction of having founded the field of institution-based addiction medicine. After 1878, references to Turner and his asylum rarely appeared in the *Journal of Inebriety*, and then primarily through the pen of his most ardent defender, T. D. Crothers. As the field continued to evolve, Turner spent most of his later life in strident defense of his work in New York, but one has the feeling that few cared to listen. Binghamton, New York, the field of addiction medicine, and the country were all moving forward to seek their own destinies.

So what is Turner's legacy viewed in retrospect from the twenty-first century? Progressive thinkers of the late eighteenth and early nineteenth centuries—Rush, Woodward, Todd—had called for the creation of special institutions for the care of the drunkard, but it required a special man of action to bring this idea to life. Although Turner made no lasting contributions to the understanding and treatment of inebriety, he was just such a man of action. His contributions were practical rather than theoretical.

The concept of inebriety as a treatable disease would have remained just an idea if Turner, or someone of his temperament, had not founded an institution in which this hypothesis could be tested. Turner had the foresight and the fortitude to sustain the struggle to open the first medically oriented institution for the treatment of addiction. In spite of his fall, he also exerted an enormous influence on others with whom he worked— particularly T. D. Crothers, who went on to be a dominant figure in the American Association for the Study and Cure of Inebriety.

Among the many addiction treatment institutions in the nineteenth century and many innovations in both clinical technology and the management of treatment institutions, what most distinguishes the New York State Inebriate Asylum was that it was the first in the world to operationalize Benjamin Rush's contention that chronic drunkenness was a medical disorder whose treatment should be the province of the physician. The asylum realized the medical conception of inebriety and placed a medical superintendent at the center of its treatment philosophy and procedures. In the intervening years, American culture and American physicians have vacillated on the claim that severe and persistent alcohol and drug problems are the province of medicine and the physician. But if one were to inquire when institution-based addiction medicine began, the answer would be clear and unequivocal: the opening of the New York State Inebriate Asylum.

A Cautionary Tale

Just as Turner's personal rise and fall constitute a cautionary tale for pioneers in emerging fields, so the rise and fall of the New York State Inebriate Asylum provide a similar cautionary tale for pioneer institutions. The fate of two such organizations in the twentieth century dramatize this point.

Synanon, the first ex-addict-directed therapeutic community, founded by Charles Dederich in 1958, rose to prominence in the 1960s.[9] One of the most widely lauded and rapidly growing treatment institutions, it was nonetheless plagued with internal problems that led to its eventual failure in a wave of accusations of unethical and illegal conduct. Dederich himself was arrested, fined, and placed on five years' probation for solicitation of assault and conspiracy to commit murder. Neither he nor his institution were ever able to restore their reputations. Synanon did launch new generations of therapeutic communities that spread across America and the world and that still serve today as major resources for the treatment of addiction. Like the New York State Inebriate Asylum, Synanon's historical significance is in the larger field it helped to launch, even in the face of its own demise.

In 1959, Lutheran General Hospital in Park Ridge, Illinois, recruited Dr. Nelson Bradley from Willmar State Hospital in Minnesota to adapt the "Minnesota Model" of chemical dependency treatment to a community hospital. Following years of successful operation, that project led to the creation of a new corporate entity, Parkside Medical Services, with the vision of replicating the Lutheran General alcoholism treatment model across the country. At its height, Parkside owned or managed more than seventy programs in twenty states, with a treatment capacity of more than 2,000 beds, more than 2,500 employees, and an annual income of more than $220 million. And yet in 1993 this largest private provider of addiction treatment services in the United States collapsed.[10]

Though quite different in particulars, the stories of Synanon and Parkside have elements reminiscent of the rise and fall of the New York State Inebriate Asylum. Synanon and the asylum suffered from charismatic and autocratic leadership, cultlike isolation from the outside world, and the exploitation of institutional resources for personal gain. Parkside and the asylum shared the experience of wrenching ideological splits between their executives and their governing boards, a loss of their founding visions, and a distortion of institutional values.

A third way in which the story in this book may serve as a cautionary tale concerns the fate of the entire nineteenth-century treatment movement that Turner initiated. This movement continued to flourish after the closure of the New York State Inebriate Asylum, only to become extinct early in the twentieth century. Its dramatic disappearance raises a most provocative question: Could the national network of addiction treatment built during the twentieth century suffer a similar fate? History suggests caution in taking for granted that today's addiction treatment resources will inevitably be here tomorrow. An earlier such network of treatment institutions once thrived and then died, its very existence unknown to many of today's treatment providers.

Although the modern system of addiction treatment is more deeply

embedded, enjoying more cultural and financial support than its predecessor, factors that contributed to the demise of nineteenth-century treatment are still relevant: (1) waning support for medical approaches to the
resolution of alcohol and other drug problems; (2) unexpected economic
downturns that rapidly eroded private and public financial support for inebriate homes and asylums; (3) the failure of the field to evaluate and, professionally and publicly, justify itself; (4) ethical abuses that damaged the
reputation of the treatment field; and (5) the failure to address problems
of leadership development and leadership succession. Combinations of
the same factors could prove lethal to modern addiction treatment.

The Fate of a Concept

The disease concept—the centerpiece of the New York State Inebriate
Asylum and the nineteenth-century inebriety treatment movement in
general—could not sustain itself as an organizing construct to address
America's alcohol and other drug addiction problems, and yet this concept
refused to die. It reemerged in the mid-twentieth century as an enabling
idea, instrumental to moving alcoholics out of the criminal justice system
and into hospitals and newly configured treatment agencies.

Arguments over the disease concept have changed but little between
the nineteenth and twenty-first centuries. Advocates passionately pro-
claim that it has opened the doors of health care institutions to alcoholics
and provided a framework for professionalized treatment, as well as a
foundation for personal recovery. They claim, in short, that the disease
concept is true and that it works. Critics vociferously claim that the disease concept should be abandoned because it is scientifically indefensible
and because it fails to account for a wide spectrum of alcohol- and drug-
related problems or to provide an empowering framework for resolving
those problems at a personal level. They claim, in short, that it is not true
and that it does not work. Advocates and critics have for over two centuries
disagreed about (1) the etiology, course, and outcome of alcohol and other
drug problems; (2) the relative effectiveness of mutual aid and professionally directed treatment; (3) the role of coercion in treatment and recovery; (4) the usefulness or harmfulness of the stigma associated with
excessive alcohol or drug use; and (5) questions of personal responsibility
regarding the behavior of the addict.

Most striking about this concept historically, despite these disagreements, is its endurance within American culture. As William White has put it, "This disease concept has survived more than two hundred years of attacks from theologians, philosophers, reformers, psychiatrists, psychologists, and sociologists, and yet continues to survive. This suggests that, as a people, we have both an individual and collective need for this concept to be 'true,' regardless of its scientific status. This truth may be more metaphoric than scientific. Science is unlikely to destroy the popularity of the disease concept, but a better metaphor could."[11]

Social Policy Then and Now

In the end, the New York Inebriate Asylum failed at multiple levels. Although Turner's contention that inebriety was a disease requiring and worthy of medical treatment attracted many patients, those same patients (and their families) bristled at Turner's demands for prolonged institutionalization and restriction of their movement beyond the hospital grounds. The asylum's clinicians formulated no lasting words or metaphors to allow inebriates and their families to make sense of their situation; sense-making tools came from others before and after the Binghamton experiment. In spite of its promises to ameliorate the community's alcohol-related problems, there is little evidence that the New York State Inebriate Asylum achieved that goal. In the year of its closing it was attacked as "a hotel for the entertainment of wealthy inebriates"–a charge predictive of contemporary criticisms that private treatment programs have become sanctuaries for celebrities to escape the consequences of their latest indiscretions and rest up for their next binge. However much the asylum may have helped individual inebriates, it did not, in the eyes of community leaders, dramatically reduce the problems associated with public drunkenness. It failed to establish and sustain its niche among competing claims for the management of addiction. This was to a great extent a failure of leadership, as other inebriate asylums did emerge and sustain themselves long after the Binghamton facility closed. But the failure of the Binghamton experiment can also be viewed in the context of a larger policy debate.

No strategy to resolve alcohol and other drug problems has ever fully succeeded. These problems, though rising and falling in prevalence and though resolved by some at an individual level, have never ceased to exact their personal and social toll. Their intractability has continued in the face of wildly varying social responses, and all the prominent strategies have fallen short of their promises.[12] Ambivalence has characterized American responses to every prevailing model of conceptualizing and solving these problems.

The New York State Inebriate Asylum represented a bold proposal in transinstitutionalization: the transfer of cultural ownership of a problem from one major social institution to another. Turner was proposing that the problem of inebriety be transferred from the arenas of religion, morality, and law to the arena of medicine. The difficulty is that none of these arenas has been able to prevent or eliminate alcohol and other drug problems at the multiple levels such resolution would require. Any organizing model purporting to resolve problems of psychoactive drug consumption (and any institution employing such a model) must work at such multiple levels. It must function as both a preventive and a rehabilitative device for individuals and families. It must provide methods of understanding and intervention for those professionals given ownership of the problem. It must provide local communities and the society at large with a way to reduce threats to public health and social order stemming from alcohol and other drug use and to guide the stewardship of resources toward this goal. The failure of any model to succeed simultaneously at all these levels has meant that any prevailing model is inherently unstable and that cyclical shifts from one model to another are the norm. Medicalized treatment, even when used as a major strategy for the resolution of alcoholism and drug addiction, has always held a probationary status within the culture. As it ascends in prominence, countervailing forces always seem to push problem definition and resolution back into the religious, moral, and criminal arenas.

The New York State Inebriate Asylum and the larger treatment movement of which it was a part marked a brief experiment in the destigmatization, decriminalization, and medicalization of alcohol and other drug problems. But while these very experiments were under way, cultural forces were afoot that led to an even more extreme pendulum swing toward restigmatization, recriminalization, and demedicalization. Long after Turner's institution had closed, the larger inebriety treatment movement collapsed under the weight of these shifting public attitudes and policies.

The history of the New York State Inebriate Asylum unfolded within a larger debate over how the causes of alcohol and other drug problems were to be defined. The policy cycles of the nineteenth century were replicated in the twentieth. Following the collapse of nineteenth-century treatment institutions between 1900 and 1920, responsibility for the control of alcoholics and addicts was shifted to local jails, inebriate penal colonies, state and federal prisons, state psychiatric hospitals, and the "foul wards" of large urban hospitals. Then reform movements of the 1940s and 1950s laid the foundation for landmark legislation out of which flowed public and private money that created a national network of addiction treatment institutions. These achieved considerable success in (re)destigmatizing addiction and diverting addicts from the criminal justice system to systems of medical and social rehabilitation.

Nevertheless, differences between the branches of nineteenth-century inebriety and temperance movements continue today: Are the problems rooted within the unique vulnerability of a minority of consumers (a problem of personal vulnerability) or, rather, in the psychoactive substances themselves and the industries that promote them (a problem of institutional culpability)?

If there is any model offering an alternative to this dualism, it is what has been christened the public health model. This approach seeks to (1) lower or manage the vulnerabilities of individuals; (2) manage the packaging, promotion, and availability of addictive substances; and (3) shape the physical and cultural environment surrounding their use in ways that minimize personal risks and social costs. The public health model may provide one of the few avenues of escape from America's cycle of polarization between narrow medical models on the one hand and punitive moral and criminal models on the other.

A Continuing Story

Replicating the policy shifts in the late nineteenth century, the rebirth of a medical model of addiction treatment in the 1960s and 1970s was followed in the 1980s by a backlash philosophy of "zero tolerance." Medical metaphors were replaced by military metaphors as alcoholics and addicts again were characterized as dangerous threats to community life who deserved sequestration and punishment. Not surprisingly, however, as the jails filled in the 1980s and 1990s, signs of a backlash against *this* approach were evident in voter referendums pushing treatment as an alternative to prison and in hybrid models of "therapeutic jurisprudence" such as the "drug court" movement. There is a growing disillusionment with drug-war rhetoric and a growing public sense that our efforts to incarcerate our way out of drug problems has failed. The call for a renewed focus on the power of treatment and personal recovery is gaining momentum.

A new recovery advocacy movement is attempting to reinstill cultural hope for recovery from addiction and to reanchor placement of alcohol and other drug problems in the medical and public health arenas. Organizationally, this movement is made up of local chapters of the National Council on Alcoholism and Drug Dependence that are attempting to recapture their community education and advocacy roots, new grassroots recovery advocacy programs, abstinence-based religious and cultural revitalization efforts, and survivor groups (parents who have experienced the addiction-related deaths of their children). These organizations are seeking to assess recovery needs within local communities, increase the quality and accessibility of treatment and recovery resources, reduce the stigma attached to addiction via professional and community education, advocate pro-recovery laws and social policies, and promote a recovery research agenda. The core ideas of the movement are somewhat different from those used by Turner or within the alcoholism movement of the mid-twentieth century. Rather than focusing on the nature of the disorder ("inebriety/alcoholism is a disease") or the nature of its resolution ("treatment works"), the new grassroots organizations are proclaiming that recovery is a reality in the lives of hundreds of thousands of individuals, families, and communities. They are celebrating the variety of recovery experiences ("many pathways to recovery") and emphasizing, in the spirit of Dr. Albert Day, that recovery is a voluntary process that can give back to individuals, families, and communities what addiction has taken.

The new recovery advocacy movement is evident in the increased number and swelling memberships of these grassroots organizations and in the growing visibility of their activities, from a national antistigma media campaign to their creation of local recovery homes and recovery support services to their hosting of large recovery celebration events to their growing sophistication in political advocacy. The energy generated by this movement is in many ways a counterpart to the energy of the Washingtonian movement that inspired the New York State Inebriate Asylum, and the movement is in many ways historically linked to this institution whose story we have explored. It is linked not to Turner's vision of sequestration and control, however, but to Day's vision of mutual support within a community of recovering people. The new recovery advocacy movement provides not a blanket support for treatment but instead a call that treatment institutions reconnect to their historical roots and mission, that treatment reconnect to the larger and more enduring process of addiction recovery, and that treatment institutions reconnect to the communities out of which they were born.[15]

Particular social reformers and particular treatment institutions may rise and fall, but the larger recovery movement is unrelenting in its historical momentum. Since the mid-eighteenth century, mutual aid groups for addiction recovery and medically and religiously oriented addiction treatment institutions have experienced numerous cycles of vitality, decline, and renewal. When systems of mutual support and institutional care collapse, recovering people and their families and visionary professionals build new systems of support and care upon the ashes of what came before. Each new generation of support structures serves to widen further the doorway of entry into recovery. Efforts to salvage alcoholics and addicts have been as ever-present in American history as efforts to stigmatize and punish them. Should the present system of addiction treatment collapse, out of that vacuum of need would emerge new recovery movements spawning new visionary reformers and new social institutions of care for those shackled in destructive relationships with alcohol and other drugs. In some form, Turner and the "Drunkard's Refuge" will exist in America's future as well as in its past.

Notes

Chapter 1

1. W. R. Rorabaugh, *The Alcoholic Republic: An American Tradition* (Oxford: Oxford University Press, 1979); A. M. Winkler, "Drinking on the American Frontier," *Quarterly Journal of Studies on Alcohol* 29 (1968): 413–45.

2. Mark Edward Lender and James Kirby Martin, *Drinking in America* (New York: Free Press, 1982).

3. Harry Gene Levine, "The Discovery of Addiction: Changing Conceptions of Habitual Drunkenness in America," *Journal of Studies on Alcohol* 39, no. 2 (1978): 143–74.

4. Anthony Benezet, *The Mighty Destroyer Displayed, in Some Account of the Dreadful Havock Made by the Mistaken Use as Well as Abuse of Distilled Spiritous Liquors* (Philadelphia: Joseph Crukshank, 1774).

5. Benjamin Rush, *An Inquiry into the Effect of Ardent Spirits upon the Human Body and Mind, with an Account of the Means of Preventing and of the Remedies for Curing Them*, 8th rev. ed. (Brookfield: E. Merriam, 1814).

6. Benjamin Rush, "Plan for an Asylum for Drunkards to Be Called the Sober House" (1810), in *The Autobiography of Benjamin Rush*, ed. G. Corner (Princeton: Princeton University Press, 1948).

7. Lyman Beecher, *Six Sermons on Intemperance*, (New York: American Tract Society, 1827), 38.

8. Samuel Woodward, *Essays on Asylums for Inebriates* (Worcester, Mass., 1838).

9. Similar changes in the perception of drunkenness were happening in England and Europe. Perhaps most significant were the writings of the English physician Thomas Trotter, whose 1804 *Essay, Medical, Philosophical, and Chemical, on Drunkenness and Its Effects on the Human Body* (London: Longman, Hurst,

Reese & Orme) declared: "In medical language, I consider drunkenness, strictly speaking, to be a disease produced by a remote cause in giving birth to actions and movements in a living body that disorders the function of health."

10. William L. White, "Addiction as a Disease: The Birth of a Concept," *Counselor* 1, no. 1 (2000): 46–51, 73.

11. Magnus Huss, *Alcoholismus chronicus: Chronisk alcoholisjudkom: Ett bidrag till dyskrasiarnas känndom* (Stockholm: Bonner/Norstedt, 1849).

12. . William Sweetser, *A Dissertation on Intemperance* (1928), in *Nineteenth Century Medical Attitudes toward Alcohol Addiction*, ed. G. Grob (New York: Arno Press, 1981), 98.

13. Dr. Springwater, *The Cold-Water-Man* (Albany, NY: Packard & Van Benthuysen, 1832), 24.

14. J. E. Todd, *Drunkenness a Vice, Not a Disease* (Hartford, Conn.: Case, Lockwood & Brainard, 1882), 12–13.

15. C. W. Earle, "The Opium Habit," *Chicago Medical Review* 2 (1880): 442–46, 493–98.

16. David J. Rothman, *The Discovery of the Asylum: Social Order and Disorder in the New Republic* (Boston: Little, Brown, 1971).

17. James Baumohl and Robin Room, "Inebriety, Doctors, and the State: Alcoholism Treatment Institutions before 1940," in *Recent Developments in Alcoholism*, vol. 5, ed. M. Galanter (New York: Plenum, 1987).

18. On these early alcoholic mutual aid societies, see William L. White, "Pre-AA Alcoholic Mutual Aid Societies," *Alcoholism Treatment Quarterly* 19, no. 1 (2001): 1–21.

19. Leonard U. Blumberg and William L. Pittman, *Beware the First Drink!: The Washington Temperance Movement and Alcoholics Anonymous* (Seattle, Wash.: Glen Abbey Books, 1991); "A Member," *The Foundation, Progress, and Principles of the Washington Temperance Society of Baltimore* (Baltimore, Md.: John D. Toy, 1842).

20. See John B. Gough, An *Autobiography* (Boston: self-published, 1845), and William George Hawkins, *Life of John H. W. Hawkins* (Boston: John P. Jewett, 1859). Other Washingtonian material is collected in *Drunkard's Progress: Narratives of Addiction, Despair, and Recovery*, ed. John W. Crowley (Baltimore, Md.: Johns Hopkins University Press, 1999).

21. This brief synopsis of nineteenth-century addiction treatment is drawn from William L. White, *Slaying the Dragon: The History of Addiction Treatment and Recovery in America* (Bloomington, Ill.: Chestnut Health Systems, 1998).

22. For a detailed account of McAuley's work, see Arthur Bonner, *Jerry McAuley and His Mission* (Neptune, NJ: Loizeaux Brothers, 1967).

23. A well-researched article on the patent medicine addiction cures is William Helfand, "Selling Addiction Cures," *Transactions and Studies of the College of Physicians of Philadelphia*, ser. 5, 43 (December 1996): 85–108.

24. *Proceedings 1870–1875, American Association for the Cure of Inebriety* (New York: Arno Press, 1981).

25. For texts illustrating the mainstream AACI view of the disease concept of inebriety, see Thomas D. Crothers, *The Disease of Inebriety from Alcohol, Opium and Other Narcotic Drugs: Its Etiology, Pathology, Treatment, and Medico-legal Relations* (New York: E. B. Treat, 1893); and Joseph Parrish, *Alcoholic Inebriety: From a Medical Standpoint* (Philadelphia: P. Blakiston, 1883).

26. *Twelfth Annual Report of the Franklin Reformatory Home for Inebriates* (Philadelphia: Treager & Lamb, 1884).

Chapter 2

1. See J. Edward Turner's self-published *History of the First Inebriate Asylum in the World* (New York, 1888). We have relied heavily on this source in the account that follows. Quotations are hereafter cited in the text and notes by use of the abbreviation *H*.

2. Biographical details are taken primarily from the remembrances of T. D. Crothers, Turner's protégé and defender. Although Crothers was partisan, and although some minor errors may be detected in his accounts, we are assuming that they are generally reliable. See his "Sketch of the Late Dr. J. Edward Turner, the Founder of Inebriate Asylums," *Quarterly Journal of Inebriety* 11 (October 1889): 301–12; and his "Memorial Address on Dr. Turner's Life and Work," *Alienist and Neurologist* 31 (February 1910): 1–20 (hereafter cited respectively as *S* and *MA*). We have also drawn upon a paper about Turner presented by one of his descendants, Madeline Turner Egerton, to the Wilton (Connecticut) Historical Society in February 1952; the typescript is held by the Broome County Historical Society, Binghamton, NY, and cited as "Egerton typescript."

3. Crothers reports that Turner wrote "a two-page tract, on the morbid anatomy and pathology [of inebriety], published in 1848, of only historic interest at this time," and that he later issued an address given before the asylum's board of directors at its second meeting, 20 December 1854: "The title was *The History and Pathology of Inebriety*. In many respects it was a very notable paper. His description of dypsomania and the allied diseases of inebriety and his distinction of the insanity of inebriety (the latter being the first reference to this form of inebriety), all indicated a very clear conception of the subject" (*S*, 307). This address is reprinted in *H*, 21–42.

4. John Kobler, *Ardent Spirits: The Rise and Fall of Prohibition* (New York: Putnam, 1973), 76.

5. Neal Dow, *The Reminiscences of Neal Dow: Recollections of Eighty Years* (Portland, Maine: Evening Press, 1898), 167, 157–58. See also Kobler, *Ardent Spirits*, 76.

6. Locke quoted in Dow, *Reminiscences,* 172. Locke, better known in his lyceum

circuit persona, Petroleum V. Nasby, was an ardent and popular crusader for prohibition.

7. In his *Reminiscences* (198), Dow suggests that the first temperance society in Maine was established in New Sharon in 1827, with several others following in rapid succession. But Ernest H. Cherrington, *The Evolution of Prohibition in the United States of America* (Westerville, Ohio: American Issue Press, 1920), 78, notes the founding of the three earlier groups.

8. Lender and Martin, *Drinking in America*, 44.

9. Dow, *Reminiscences*, 206.

10. Norman H. Clark, *Deliver Us from Evil: An Interpretation of American Prohibition* (New York: Norton, 1976), 40.

11. "He [Turner] was repeatedly asked to take part in reform work and his answer was 'restore the body, correct the surroundings, and then reform work will be natural and real, because the soil on which it must grow has been cultivated'" (*MA*, 4).

12. Theodore L. Mason, "Anniversary Address of the AACI," *Journal of Inebriety* 1 (December 1879): 8.

13. On the English advocates of the disease model of inebriety, see Anya Taylor, *Bacchus in Romantic England: Writers and Drink, 1780–1830* (New York: St. Martin's, 1999), 11–28.

14. Rothman, *Discovery of the Asylum*, xiii, xviii.

15. The number and sequence of Turner's European sojourns is uncertain. Crothers notes his travels in 1843 and 1848–49 but makes no mention of a second trip to England. The Egerton typescript, however, refers to his English tour in 1850 as his "second" European excursion, making no mention of any 1843 trip. Turner was presented at court, according to Egerton; lacking the proper attire, having brought only a Prince Albert coat with him to Europe, Turner simply "pinned the tails up and bowed with the usual aplomb!"

16. To the New York state legislature, Turner reported, with his usual exactitude: "We have traveled by railway one hundred and fifty thousand, two hundred and twenty-three miles; by steamships twelve thousand, six hundred and seventy-three miles; by diligence, six thousand, five hundred and eleven miles; and have walked more than five thousand miles"–nearly 175,00 miles in all. See *Second Annual Report of the New York State Inebriate Asylum* (Albany, NY: Comstock & Cassidy, 1863), 1.

17. The charter is reprinted in its entirety in *H*, 59–61.

18. The ideal asylum, according to Rothman, "was to have a country location with ample grounds, to sit on a low hillside with an unobstructed view of a surrounding landscape. The scene ought to be tranquil, natural, and rural, not tumultuous and urban" (*Discovery of the Asylum*, 138). The Binghamton site fit these specifications to a tee.

19. Rothman points out that "almost all the institutions constructed after 1820

were located at a short distance from an urban center" (*Discovery of the Asylum,* 141).

20. Karla M. Eisch, "The New York State Inebriate Asylum," *Broome County Historical Society Newsletter,* Summer 1994, 2.

21. Rothman, *Discovery of the Asylum,* 141.

22. Eisch reports that the cornerstone, placed at the northeast corner, contained fifty-five items, "including a copy of each Binghamton newspaper, an old Japanese coin and an Indian Pipe of Peace" ("New York State Inebriate Asylum," 3). During the centennial of the Binghamton Psychiatric Center in 1981, however, the cornerstone could not be located.

23. Turner related a relevant conversation with Reuben Hyde Walworth, second president of the board: "'It is my humble opinion,' said the Chancellor, 'that if you found the Inebriate Asylum, you will establish the fact that inebriety is a constitutional and hereditary disease, out of which grows a form of insanity more dangerous than that of the class which is now confined in our insane asylums. You will be able to sweep away the legal fallacy of holding one human being responsible for murder committed under the influence of a brain diseased by alcohol, and at the same time not permitting another laboring under the same disease, to testify in the witness-box, nor to be held responsible for contracts made under the same diseased conditions" (*H,* 155–56).

24. Eisch, "New York State Inebriate Asylum," 3. Turner itemizes the losses as follows: the machinery in the carpenter's shop; 250,000 board feet of cherry and other hardwoods; fifty cherry bedsteads; fifty wardrobes; the staircases of the transept; the finished woodwork for the south wing (*H,* 271).

25. In recent years, strong efforts have been made by the Preservation Association of the Southern Tier (PAST) to save the asylum building, which has been vacant since 1993. It was placed on the National Register of Historic Places in August 1996 and listed as a National Historic Landmark in November 1997. As of February 2001 it became an official project of the Save America's Treasures program, which provides federal restoration funds on a matching basis.

26. Eisch, "New York State Inebriate Asylum," 3.

27. Rothman, *Discovery of the Asylum,* 134.

28. Ibid., 153.

29. Ibid., 133.

30. Ibid., 142–43.

Chapter 3

1. Eisch, "New York State Inebriate Asylum," 40.

2. According to Dr. Willard Parker's report to the state in 1867, twenty-six patients were admitted during 1866, and no more than thirty-four were present at any one time. Since opening in 1864, the asylum had treated eighty-two in-

mates in all: "No patient was received for less than one year, and payment for the first six months was required in advance. Only ten out of the whole number remained for a year, the remainder leaving, some at the end of two, others at four, others at six, and others at eight or nine months." According to Turner, who counted eighty-five patients, more than half were between the ages of twenty-five and thirty-five; thirty-six were single, thirty-four married, and the rest widowed or divorced. Fifty-eight were "constitutional" inebriates; twenty-seven, "hereditary." Fifty-seven were steady drinkers; ten, periodics. Forty-five had suffered delirium tremens; twelve, convulsions. Sixty-seven also used tobacco; five, opium and alcohol; two, opium alone. The patients' occupations ranged widely across the professional categories; the largest groups were businessmen, clerks, and military officers. Eleven "gentlemen" were present, along with one "gentleman farmer." There was also a smattering of working-class men: two seamen, one cashier, one blacksmith. Nine of the patients were registered under assumed names to conceal their identities even from the physicians (*H*, 209–11, 216). The complete roster of Turner's patients, including their identities, is in the files of the Broome County Historical Society.

3. *Fourth Annual Report of the New York State Inebriate Asylum* (Albany: O. Wendell, 1866), 42–43.

4. Ibid., 14–15.

5. Ibid., 15–16.

6. One of the few opium addicts to be treated at Binghamton later wrote of his experience under Dr. Daniel G. Dodge, one of Turner's successors. About the search-and-seizure policy, he smirked: "The gentlemen, however, are usually far too shrewd to become the victims of any such unlucky *contretemps* as this. Any one carrying liquor from the village [such visits were allowed after Turner's departure], unless he has already got too much of it inside of him to know what he is about, will be likely to anticipate any such summary proceeding as this by leaving his flask behind a stump or in a fence-corner at the bottom of the hill." Such stratagems were unnecessary for a dope addict, he added, because "I could conceal enough of the drug under my thumb-nail to keep me happy for 24 hours." J. C. L., "Curing the Opium Habit: The Treatment in the Binghamton Asylum," letter to the *New York Times,* undated clipping, Broome County Historical Society.

7. See the affidavits, in Turner's hand, in the Broome County Historical Society collection.

8. "Shall We Close the Harbor?" unidentified newspaper clipping dated 22 January 1879, Broome County Historical Society.

9. Senta Rypins, "Joseph Turner and the First Inebriate Asylum," *Quarterly Journal of Studies on Alcohol* 10 (June 1949): 130. Turner's roster of patients includes "gentlemen" with such notable names as Tiffany and Roosevelt.

10. Entry on Willard Parker in Mark Edward Lender, *Dictionary of American*

Temperance Biography (Westport, Conn.: Greenwood Press, 1984), 385–86. Other details are also taken from this source.

11. In the first of two surviving letters from Parker to Turner, the surgeon took a friendly tone: "I appreciate your situation," he wrote, "& I *will help*." Letter of 18 July 1865, Broome County Historical Society.

12. In the second of his surviving letters to Turner, Parker reiterated his concerns: "I am anxious to know how you are progressing in the completion of the asylum. . . . Some who have seen the Institution and who have some [illegible] say the whole concern is a failure and complain that its patients get out, procure spirits. They say much money has been expended and no account rendered. I want to see you, when in the City and we will see what can be done. I think the great mistake has been in the admission of patients before one wing was completed and the library, chapel &c were more nearly finished. The patients now feel they are conferring a favor. Whereas the friends should feel they were the *obliged* party. We will see what it is best to do about taking more patients." Letter of 9 September 1865, Broome County Historical Society.

13. Willard Parker, "Inebriety as a Disease," unidentified newspaper clipping dated 12 February 1879, Broome County Historical Society.

14. Parker's affidavit appeared in the *Norwalk (Connecticut) Gazette* 51 (27 October 1868): 1, Broome County Historical Society. Its publication was apparently arranged by Dr. Gardiner, who had recently won acquittal on the arson charges brought by Parker and his allies. Gardiner was sarcastically offering a $1,000 reward, fronted by "ten prominent gentlemen" in New York City, to the first "three honorable men who will prove to the world which of the two following contradictory affidavits of Dr. Willard Parker is a true history of the Inebriate Asylum, in order that the world may be enlightened as to the utility and practicability of building more inebriate asylums." Along with the hostile deposition of 1868, Gardiner presented a far more sanguine assessment of Turner's leadership which Parker had given on 8 January 1867 in an official report to the state. Needless to say, Gardiner did not expect three men – or even one – to come forward to collect the reward.

15. This is Turner's only mention of his family in the *History*. From material in his papers it may be inferred that two younger children, Gertrude and Joseph, were five and three respectively in 1881, when ground was broken for the National Woman's Hospital in Wilton (see *H*, 476). Any children who would have been babies in 1866 have not been identified.

16. Rypins, "Joseph Turner and the First Inebriate Asylum," 130.

17. See letters from Birdsall to Turner, 7 and 24 January 1865; and Samuel Fitch to Turner, 7 July 1865. Birdsall, it seems, was not the only new trustee with a dubious reputation. Another citizen had complained of William R. Osborn: "I cannot understand why a man like Mr Osborn should take an interest in a great

moral reform enterprise when he takes a lively interest in visiting (when he is in New York) the fashionable whore houses of the city." J. P. Freeman to Turner, 2 February 1865. All these letters are in the files of the Broome County Historical Society.

18. Embroidered in transmission through the gossip mill, the litany of Turner's sins was sometimes expanded to include not only arson, embezzlement, defalcation, theft, and bigamy but also religious infidelity and even murder (see *H*, 376, 409). The charge of infidelity is explained by Turner's refusal, consistent with his general exclusion of outsiders, to allow Christian revivalists access to the patients for purposes of working cures by conversion. The charge of murder is completely unaccountable.

19. Turner was convinced that Parton was in collusion with Parker. During his later troubles in Connecticut, when Parton's article resurfaced, Turner evidently wrote him to demand the truth. Parton's reply (in full): "I was not employed by any party or parties to write the piece to which you refer in yours of Oct. 24th. It was my own idea." Letter of 28 October 1885, Broome County Historical Society.

20. James Parton, "Inebriate Asylums, and a Visit to One," collected in Parton, *Smoking and Drinking* (Boston: Ticknor & Fields, 1868), 113–17. Turner reprinted the entire damning passage in *H*, 272–76. Turner also quoted one indignant mother who believed that the offensive name of the asylum was scaring off potential patients, lest they be marked as madmen: "If the naming of the Asylum had been chosen with any degree of interest and sympathy for the inebriate or for his friends, it would have been called a Home for Inebriates, and this name would have led its founder to have made it more like a home than a jail." Against such objections, Turner fulminated: "To call a pest-house a church is a fraud which would not change the loathsomeness of small-pox, its treatment or even its restraint. To name a yellow fever hospital a home, would be a trick which would not change the control of yellow fever or make it less than an epidemic. To christen a lunatic asylum a college, would not by this device induce more lunatics to enter its halls, diminish its restraint over its patients, or exclude from its wards its medical treatment. To name an inebriate asylum a home, with all its appliances to control and medically treat successfully the suicidal, homicidal dipsomaniac, (which all inebriates become before their friends send them to the inebriate hospital) would be, to my mind, a fraud upon frauds" (*H*, 189–90).

21. Quoted in Parton, *Smoking and Drinking*, 115–16 n.

22. These aspects of the Battle of Binghamton–the proxy fight of 1867 and the severance settlement for Turner–lead into a thicket of legalistic wrangling about corporate rules of order and the proper basis for figuring Turner's due compensation–all tangential to our purposes here. The interested reader should consult Turner's *History*. On balance, it seems unfair to suggest that Turner came out of the disaster bearing "enormous booty," and there is no evidence–only Parker's

and Birdsall's suspicions—that Turner had been stealing the asylum's funds all along.

23. Eisch, "New York State Inebriate Asylum," 4. Eisch points out a discrepancy in dating this fire: Turner's *History* says 1869; the 1870 annual report says March 1870. We assume the later date to be correct.

24. Turner to his mother, 4 May 1873, Broome County Historical Society.

25. Rypins, "Joseph Turner and the First Inebriate Asylum," 132. A document in the Broome County Historical Society files shows that Turner hired an attorney, A. N. Cole, on 3 February 1876. A copy of the defendants' reply to the suit is also among Turner's papers.

26. Turner purchased a fifty-acre farm in Wilton in September 1867, and he evidently started a dairy. But along with his old associate T. Jefferson Gardiner, Turner also treated a few inebriates privately at his twelve-room home, having obtained from the state of Connecticut, in May 1868, a resolution incorporating "Turner's Dipsomaniac Retreat." A copy of the document is held by the Broome County Historical Society.

27. Turner evidently gave part of his farm for the project and sold the rest of it to the hospital corporation.

28. "Female Inebriety," unidentified clipping, c. 1880, Broome County Historical Society.

29. One of Turner's New York friends, Dr. Frank H. Hamilton, suspected "that Mr. Collyer's opposition to the charter of the Hospital was prompted by Dr. Willard Parker," and he vilified Collyer as "a character that wore the face of a woman with the body of a hyena" (quoted in *H*, 490). The deeper meaning of this oblique insult is not immediately apparent, although it seems to carry homophobic overtones. Nor is the significance of the following sentence, which Turner hand-canceled with hash marks in every known copy of the *History:* "Collyer's complications at the island of St. Domingo, his imprisonment and its history, can be found at the State Department at Washington, D.C." We suppose that Collyer got himself entangled in some sort of scandal.

30. Parker had died, in his eighty-fourth year, on 25 April 1884. Turner implies here that the hostile senator's "manner and talk" had literally been "imbued with Dr. Parker's spirit," as if Turner's nemesis, still plaguing him from beyond the grave, had uncannily been reincarnated in the person of R. J. Walsh. It may be, in fact, that one of Parker's last living acts had been to incite Collyer against Turner. In circulating Parton's *Atlantic Monthly* article, Collyer explicitly invoked Parker's authority: "No one in this country stands higher for benevolence and professional ability than the great surgeon, Dr. Willard Parker, and his statements in regard to the New York State Inebriate Asylum can be relied upon as being truthful" (quoted in *H*, 481).

31. Official transcript, Broome County Historical Society.

32. Egerton typescript.

33. A copy of Mrs. Turner's letter is in the Broome County Historical Society files.

34. Inscription quoted in Egerton transcript. See also newspaper clippings, Broome County Historical Society.

35. The most embarrassing charge against Parker, which Turner delighted to record (more than once), was that this stalwart of temperance had, since 1850, been hypocritically collecting $15,000 a year in rent as the proprietor of a New York City hotel where "the purest of wines and liquors" were advertised and sold. See *H*, 319, 437 n, 443–44.

36. Rypins, "Joseph Turner and the First Inebriate Asylum," 133.

Chapter 4

1. "The N.Y. Inebriate Asylum, under One Year of Good Rule," *Binghamton Democrat*, 7 May 1868, Broome County Historical Society. During all of 1868, 310 patients were eventually received, of whom "ninety-three were clerks, eighty-two merchants, sixteen farmers, fifteen lawyers, nine brokers and bankers, and twenty-eight 'independent gentlemen' of no occupation." There were also five printers, three clergymen, two physicians, two authors, two teachers, one artist, and two professional musicians. [John W. Palmer], "Our Inebriates, Harbored and Helped," *Atlantic Monthly* 24 (July 1869): 112.

2. Albert Day, *Methomania* (Boston: James Campbell, 1867), 35–36, 39.

3. Note the petty malice expressed by the *Binghamton Democrat* article in contrasting "Dr." Day to "Mr." Turner—as if the latter were not entitled to be called a physician. It was still widely believed in Binghamton that Turner's medical credentials were fraudulent. Mrs. Willard Parker, writing under the pseudonym "Truth," had published a derogatory article in 1866 in which she sneered about "this Turner calling himself doctor, though without an M.D." "The New York Inebriate Asylum and Its Failure," *Advocate and Guardian* 1 (November 1866); reprinted in *H*, 437–40. It is quite possible that Turner did not hold the degree of Medical Doctor, having neither attended college nor enrolled in a medical school. But he was licensed by the state of Maine and had practiced medicine, however briefly, in New Jersey.

4. "The New York State Inebriate Asylum," *Binghamton Daily Republican*, 1 February 1868, Broome County Historical Society. The story is marked as having been originally published in the *Rochester Express*.

5. In Boston, the Washingtonian movement spawned three boardinghouses for the shelter of inebriates. One of these, originally called the Home for the Fallen, was subsequently incorporated as the Washingtonian Home; its charter was accepted by the state of Massachusetts on 2 May 1857. In 1873, when Day returned

for his second term as superintendent, a new building was erected, and under various names the Washingtonian Home operated until 1979: the longest surviving addiction hospital in America.

6. T. D. Crothers, "The Late Dr. Albert Day: A Biographical Sketch," *Quarterly Journal of Inebriety* 18 (1896): 51. Biographical details are taken both from Crothers's article and from the entry on Day in Lender, *Dictionary of American Temperance Biography*, 128–29. That Crothers was Turner's devoted disciple adds weight to his giving priority to the Washingtonian Home over the New York State Inebriate Asylum. The charter for the asylum was granted in 1854, three years before the one for the Boston facility; thus, if chartering counts as the moment of institutional conception, then Turner's claim of founding the first inebriate "asylum" in the world may technically be valid–but only technically, since the Washingtonian Home was fully operational *as an asylum* in 1857, long before patients were admitted to the Binghamton institution in 1864. Other inebriate asylums soon followed: in Media, Pennsylvania (near Philadelphia) in 1867 and in Chicago in 1868.

7. Albert Day, "Causations of Alcoholic Inebriety, Read before the American Association for the Study and Cure of Inebriety," *Quarterly Journal of Inebriety* 13 (April 1891): 27; Day, *Methomania*, 49–50.

8. Crothers, "The Late Dr. Albert Day," 53, 54.

9. Parton, *Smoking and Drinking*, 129–30, 148–49.

10. Ibid., 128, 129, 139, 135.

11. Ibid., 138.

12. Ibid.

13. Ibid., 109.

14. [Palmer], "Our Inebriates, Harbored and Helped," 109. Parton (*Smoking and Drinking*, 126) had described the private rooms as "equal, both in size and furniture, to those of good city hotels. The arrangements for warming, lighting, washing, bathing, cooking, are such as we should expect to find in so stately an edifice."

15. The "blue-and-gold" series Palmer refers to was a popular set of English and American poets, issued in attractive uniform bindings by Ticknor & Fields, Boston's leading publisher. Although the asylum library was built to accommodate 20,000 volumes, there was a chronic shortage of books actually on the shelves. Turner and his successors were constantly appealing to subscribers and others for donations. One visitor to the asylum made such a special plea: "The principal want of the institution for the entertainment and occupation of its inmates, and which there appears no immediate means of supplying, is that necessity of every intelligent mind–a LIBRARY. Especially for a community of this kind, made up largely of persons of liberal education and originally devoted to reading and study, whose habits in these respects have been interrupted by those of different character, the value of a varied, well selected, and good sized library

cannot be too highly estimated. . . .books upon all subjects will be acceptable." John H. Griscom, "A Visit to the State Inebriate Asylum," *Independent,* 26 October 1865.

16. [Palmer], "Our Inebriates, Harbored and Helped," 110, and "Our Inebriates, Classified and Clarified," *Atlantic Monthly* 23 (April 1869): 479. J. W. Palmer's authorship of these articles has been established by Nancy Glazener in *Reading for Realism: The History of a U.S. Literary Institution, 1850–1910* (Durham, N.C.: Duke University Press, 1997). See her suggestive third chapter, "Addictive Reading and Authorship."

17. [Palmer], "Our Inebriates, Harbored and Helped," 114–15.

18. Ibid.

19. According to Turner's roster of patients, Frederick Stowe, age twenty-four, entered the asylum voluntarily on 2 May 1866; he was discharged two months later (7 July). Returning to the Asylum late in 1867, he was kept under lock and key during withdrawal. His first three months were filled with lethargy and despair, but he was assured he would recover in time. His mother took great comfort in the superintendent's reputation for working miracles: "Dr Day has saved men whom drink had reduced to maundering idiocy whom he picked up frozen in the streets and they are leading temperance men in Boston." During her visit to Binghamton she "examined piles of papers & letters from redeemed men now holding station & conducting business every where who had been wallowing brutes with this curse." Quoted in Joan D. Hedrick, *Harriet Beecher Stowe: A Life* (New York: Oxford University Press, 1994), 336. The material read by Mrs. Stowe likely came from Day's collection of progress reports. It was a custom, Parton says (*Smoking and Drinking,* 141), for former patients to write to Day "on the anniversary of their entering the Home under his management, and the reading of such letters is a highly interesting and beneficial feature of the Wednesday evening temperance meetings."

20. Parton, *Smoking and Drinking,* 141. Parton earlier (102) quotes Stowe on the tribulations of inebriety: "Many a drunkard has expended more virtue in vain endeavors to break his chain than suffices to carry an ordinary Christian to heaven." She may well have been thinking of her son's chronic inebriety–or of her daughter Georgiana's equally harrowing addiction to morphine.

21. [Palmer], "Our Inebriates, Harbored and Helped," 111. "S. T.-1860-X" was a popular patent medicine of the day; like most such elixirs, it probably contained a potent quantity of alcohol.

22. Parton, *Smoking and Drinking,* 136–38.

23. [Palmer], "Our Inebriates, Harbored and Helped," 112–13, 116.

24. Day's annual report for 1868, quoted in [Palmer], "Our Inebriates, Harbored and Helped," 114, 113.

25. Turner went on to criticize the urban location of the Boston asylum: "I would as soon think of building a mad-house in Wall Street (where the noise and excitement of speculation run rampant) for the successful treatment of the insane

broker or banker as to build an Inebriate Asylum in the city, where the fumes of distilleries and grogshops pervade the very air we breathe. Such an institution needs for its surroundings a pure country atmosphere, the sloping hill, the flowing river, the song of birds; and above all a religious, moral and intelligent community." Copy of Turner to M. M. Fisher, 23 May 1859, Broome County Historical Society. The date 1859 is problematical, however, because, although Turner specifically states that his visit occurred "last October" (i.e., October 1858), he calls the Boston institution "the Home of the Fallen" [*sic*]. But the Home for the Fallen had already become the Washingtonian Home as of May 1857, and Day was already acting as medical superintendent. We cannot account for these discrepancies except to speculate that Turner's visit actually occurred before 1857. In fact, the date on Turner's letter (a copy in his hand, not the original) could be construed to read 1854 rather than 1859, in which case, his visit would have been in October 1853—except that the institution was not officially known as the Home for the Fallen *before* 1857. The dating conundrum does not affect, in any case, the substance of Turner's remarks about the Washingtonian maltreatment (as he saw it) of inebriety.

26. Rypins, "Joseph Turner and the First Inebriate Asylum," 132.

27. "Dr. Day and the Asylum," *Binghamton Democratic Leader,* 18 March 1870, Broome County Historical Society.

28. Turner goes on, in a somewhat paranoid vein: "He [Day] then fully realized why the founder was indicted; why James Brown, the colored man, was kept at the Asylum as a defamer; why he, and all the officers of the Asylum, were instructed to state to all visitors and patients that the founder was a bad man; and why he was instructed to furnish Mr. Parton with the misrepresentations which he makes the foundation of his article in the *Atlantic Monthly*" (*H,* 271–72).

29. Rypins, "Joseph Turner and the First Inebriate Asylum," 131.

30. Quoted in "The Inebriate Asylum," *Binghamton Daily Republican,* 13 May 1870, Broome County Historical Society.

31. McFarland quoted in *H,* 429–30.

32. Edward C. Delavan to Turner, 21 September 1858 (Delavan's ellipsis), Broome County Historical Society. Many of the other letters Turner received on the occasion of breaking ground for the asylum were published in his *History.*

33. Turner, *Fourth Annual Report* (1866), 16–17.

34. Mott quoted in *H,* 20. Mott's statement was made in 1847, according to Charles J. Douglas, M.D., "Historical Notes on the Sanitorium Treatment of Alcoholism," *Medical Record* 57 (10 March 1900): 410.

35. Elisha Harris, *The Criminality of Drunkenness: Judged by the Laws of Nature,* National Temperance Society and Publication House Pamphlet no. 126 (n.p., n.d.), 1.

36. Turner reprinted Bellows's untitled address in *H,* 111–26, from which the quotations are taken.

37. We imagine that Bellows's closely reasoned argument sailed over the heads of Turner and many of the other dignitaries in 1858. Turner blandly reports that "Dr. Bellows was listened to with the utmost attention, and at the close warmly applauded" (*H*, 126). If he had followed Bellows's logic, Turner would not have shared the minister's resistance to the purely medical model to which he himself subscribed so fiercely.

38. Mott quoted in *H*, 163.

39. T. D. Crothers, "Historic Address on the Journal of Inebriety, Its Birth and Growth," *Journal of Inebriety* 19 (1897): 21, 23.

40. Orestes M. Brands, *Lessons on the Human Body: An Elementary Treatise upon Physiology, Hygiene, and the Effects of Stimulants and Narcotics on the Human System* (Boston: Leach, Shewell & Sanborn, 1883), 202.

41. Vance Thompson, *Drink and Be Sober* (New York: Moffat, Yard, 1915), 108–9.

42. [Palmer], "Our Inebriates, Classified and Clarified," 477–78.

43. [Palmer], "Our Inebriates, Harbored and Helped," 117.

44. Ibid.

45. In practice, either method seemed to work for significant numbers of patients. Various cure rates, none of which can be taken as reliable, were bandied about by Turner and Day advocates alike. Turner claimed that when he ran the asylum, "more than half of its patients were discharged cured" (*H*, 450). After Day's first year, the *Binghamton Democrat* boasted: "We know and can prove from actual statistics that more than seventy percent of those who have left the institution have been reformed, and are filling stations of honor and usefulness" ("The N.Y. Inebriate Asylum," 7 May 1868). These results, presumably, reflected *both* the Turner and Day administrations. Willard Parker asserted in 1879 ("Inebriety as a Disease") that data had been collected for the three years *after* Day's departure, showing that of the 416 former patients who responded to a survey (of 1,432 inmates actually admitted between 1870 and 1873), "*more than sixty-one percent* had remained cured." In 1891, referring to this same study of the asylum, Crothers cited different statistics but reported the same results: of 1,100 replies from friends of the 1,500 patients treated in 1868 (that is, in one year under Day), "sixty-one and a fraction per cent were still temperate and well, after a period of five years. It was a reasonable inference, that if sixty-one per cent were still restored after this interval, a large percentage would continue so through the remaining life." Crothers also cited cure statistics from other and smaller asylums in the United States and Europe, "where the number studied were limited to a few hundred or less, and the interval or time since the treatment was from four to eight years"; in these, the number reported as "free from all use of spirits" ranged from 32 to 41 percent. His conservative conclusion was that one in three inebriates could likely be cured under the conditions of the time—a rate he thought could be improved by more scientific treatment in the future. T. D.

Crothers, "Are Inebriates Curable?" *Journal of the American Medical Association* 17 (12 December 1891): 926.

46. Robinson quoted in Eisch, "New York State Inebriate Asylum," 4.

47. Crothers, "Are Inebriates Curable?" 926.

48. Details in the following paragraphs are taken from various and mostly unidentified newspaper clippings in the Broome County Historical Society collection.

49. Daniel G. Dodge, "Inebriate Asylums and Their Management," *Journal of Inebriety* 1 (June 1877): 130, 139, 144. In the annual report for 1876, Dodge similarly lamented the admission of patients suffering from advanced physical and mental deterioration.

50. "The Fifth Annual Report of the New York State Inebriate Asylum for the Year 1877," *Journal of Inebriety* 2 (September 1878): 230.

51. One newspaper story, "Why the New York Binghamton Inebriate Asylum Was a Failure" (undated clipping, Broome County Historical Society), claimed that the asylum had been "managed by nine different superintendents." If so, then some of the names have been lost. According to Turner's account, there were only six different superintendents, with Dodge serving twice. Given Turner's usual punctiliousness, we tend to accept his count as accurate.

52. Doolittle quoted in *H,* 358.

53. Turner's charges were reported in at least one newspaper: "Why the New York Binghamton Inebriate Asylum Was a Failure" cites details from the 1876 lawsuit about alleged graft among the trustees. The undated memorandum (Broome County Historical Society), written in pencil and titled "Why the Binghamton Inebriate Asylum Suspended," is apparently in Turner's hand. Stapled to the first page, however, is a brief letter (or a copy of such) from T. D. Crothers, which instructs Turner: "Keep the note I enclose you [*sic*] do not leave it in the *Editor's hands.* You know my reasons. I must keep out of all complications at present. I shall watch for its appearance next week." The authorship of the memorandum, then, is in doubt. It may have been composed by Crothers and then copied by Turner for his own records, but it sounds very much like Turner's work.

54. Bellows quoted in *H,* 400.

55. Mott quoted in *H,* 168.

Chapter 5

1. Thomas D. Crothers, "Inebriate Asylums," in *The Cyclopedia of Temperance and Prohibition* (New York: Funk & Wagnalls, 1891).

2. Thomas D. Crothers, editorial, *Journal of Inebriety* 21 (1899): 93–94.

3. For surveys documenting the dramatic decline of treatment institutions during the opening years of Prohibition, compare Horatio Pollock and Edith Furbush, "Insane, Feebleminded, Epileptics and Inebriates in Institutions in the

United States," *Mental Hygiene* 99 (1 January 1917): 548–66, with Cora F. Stoddard, "What of the Drink Cures?" *Scientific Temperance Journal,* September 1922, 55–64.

4. See Samuel Hopkins Adams, "The Scavengers," *Collier's Weekly,* 22 September 1906, 112–13 (reprinted series).

5. For a review of early alcoholic mutual aid societies, see White, "Pre-AA Alcoholic Mutual Aid Societies."

6. The history of the "modern alcoholism movement" has been captured in two well-researched dissertations: Bruce Holley Johnson, "The Alcoholism Movement in America: A Study in Cultural Innovation" (Ph.D. diss., University of Illinois, Urbana, 1973); and Ron Roizen, "The American Discovery of Alcoholism, 1933–1939" (Ph.D. diss., University of California, Berkeley, 1991).

7. See Dwight Anderson, "Alcohol and Public Opinion," *Quarterly Journal of Studies on Alcohol* 3 (1942): 376–92; Marty Mann, "Formation of a National Committee for Education on Alcoholism," *Quarterly Journal of Studies on Alcohol* 5 (1944): 354.

8. William L. White, *The Incestuous Workplace* (Center City, Minn.: Hazelden, 1997).

9. Much has been written on the turbulent history of Synanon, but two books well characterize its beginning and end: Lewis Yablonsky, *Synanon: The Tunnel Back* (Baltimore, Md.: Penguin, 1965); and Dave Mitchell, Cathy Mitchell, and Richard Ofshe, *The Light on Synanon* (New York: Seaview Books, 1980). The most comprehensive treatment of this history can be found in Rod Janzen, *The Rise and Fall of Synanon* (Baltimore, Md.: Johns Hopkins University Press, 2001).

10. A chapter detailing the history of Parkside can be found in White, *Slaying the Dragon.*

11. White, *Slaying the Dragon.* See also White, "Addiction as a Disease"; W. L. White, "The Rebirth of the Disease Concept of Alcoholism in the 20th Century," *Counselor* 1, no. 2 (2000): 62–66; White, "Addiction Disease Concept: Advocates and Critics," *Counselor* 2 (2001): 42–46; White, "A Disease Concept for the 21st Century," *Counselor* 2 (2001): 44–52.

12. For an excellent treatise on the instability in models of response to alcohol and other drug problems, see Robin Room, "Governing Images of Alcohol and Drug Problems: The Structure, Sources and Sequels of Conceptualizations of Intractable Problems" (Ph.D. diss., University of California, Berkeley, 1978).

13. See www.facesandvoicesofrecovery.org for a directory of groups. The seminal papers on the new recovery advocacy movement are posted at www. bhrm.org. See also William L. White, "A Call to Service: The New Recovery Advocacy Movement," *Counselor* 2 (2001): 64–67.

Selected Bibliography

Archival Resources

Broome County Historical Society, 185 Court Street, Binghamton, New York 13901 (607/778–3572).

Illinois Addiction Studies Archives, Chestnut Health Systems, Bloomington, Illinois 61701 (309/827–6026).

Recommended Reading on the Asylum

Brown, Edward "What Shall We Do with the Inebriate? Asylum Treatment and the Disease Concept of Alcoholism in the Late Nineteenth Century." *Journal of the History of the Behavioral Sciences* 21 (1985): 48–59.

Crothers, Thomas D. "The Pioneer Founder of America's Inebriate State Hospital." *Alienist and Neurologist* 35 (1914): 40–60.

Eisch, Karla M. "The New York State Inebriate Asylum." *Broome County Historical Society Newsletter,* Summer 1994, 1–4.

Lender, Mark Edward. "J. E. Turner." In *Dictionary of American Temperance Biography,* 491–93. Westport, Conn.: Greenwood Press, 1984.

[Palmer, J. W.] "Our Inebriates, Classified and Clarified." *Atlantic Monthly* 24: (July 1869): 109–19.

———. "Our Inebriates, Harbored and Helped." *Atlantic Monthly* 23 (April 1869).

Parton, James. "Inebriate Asylums, and a Visit to One." *Atlantic Monthly* 22 (October 1868): 385–404. Reprinted in Parton, *Smoking and Drinking,* 101–51 (Boston: Ticknor & Fields, 1868).

Proceedings 1870–1875, American Association for the Cure of Inebriates. New York: Arno Press, 1981.

Rypins, Senta. "Joseph Turner and the First Inebriate Asylum." *Quarterly Journal of Studies on Alcohol* 10 (June 1949): 127–34.

Turner, J. Edward. "A Circular, by the Superintendent, New York State Inebriate Asylum" (16 pages). 1870.

———. *History of the First Inebriate Asylum in the World.* New York: Privately printed. 1888.

———. "Superintendent's Report to the Board of Trustees," New York State Inebriate Asylum (32 pages). 1867.

Background Resources

Baumohl, James. "Inebriate Institutions in North America, 1840–1920." *British Journal of Addictions* 85 (1990): 1187–1204.

Baumohl, James, and Robin Room. "Inebriety, Doctors, and the State: Alcoholism Treatment Institutions before 1940." In *Recent Developments in Alcoholism*, ed. M. Galanter, 5:135–74. New York: Plenum Publishing, 1987.

Baumohl, James, and Sarah Tracy. "Building Systems to Manage Inebriates: The Divergent Pathways of California and Massachusetts, 1891–1920." *Contemporary Drug Problems* 21 (1994): 557–97.

Blumberg, Leon. "The American Association for the Study and Cure of Inebriety." *Alcoholism: Clinical and Experimental Research* 2 (1978): 234–40.

———. "The Institutional Phase of the Washingtonian Total Abstinence Movement: A Research Note." *Journal of Studies on Alcohol* 39 (1978): 1593.

Crothers, Thomas D. "Are Inebriates Curable?" *Journal of the American Medical Association* 17 (1891): 923–27.

———. *The Disease of Inebriety from Alcohol, Opium, and Other Narcotic Drugs: Its Etiology, Pathology, Treatment, and Medico-legal Relations.* New York: E. B. Treat, 1893.

———. *Inebriety: A Clinical Treatise on the Etiology, Symptomatology, Neurosis, Psychosis, and Treatment.* Cincinnati, Ohio: Harvey, 1911.

———. "Inebriety in Women." *Quarterly Journal of Inebriety* 2 (1878): 247–48.

———. "A Review of the History and Literature of Inebriety, the First Journal, and Its Work to Present." *Journal of Inebriety* 33 (1912): 139–51.

Crowley, John W., ed. *Drunkard's Progress: Narratives of Addiction, Despair, and Recovery.* Baltimore: Johns Hopkins University Press, 1999.

Davis, N. S. "Inebriate Asylums: The Principles That Should Govern Us in the Treatment of Inebriates and the Institutions Needed to Aid Their Restoration." *Journal of Inebriety* 2 (1877): 80–88.

Day, Albert. "Causations of Alcoholic Inebriety." *Quarterly Journal of Inebriety,* 13 (April 1891): 127.

———. *Methomania: A Treatise on Alcoholic Poisoning.* Boston: James Campbell, 1867. Reprinted in *Nineteenth-Century Medical Attitudes toward Alcoholic Addiction,* ed. G. Grob (New York: Arno Press, 1981).

Dodge, Daniel. "Inebriate Asylums and Their Management." *Quarterly Journal of Inebriety* 1 (June 1877): 126–44.

Hall, Howard R. "Professionalism, Psychology, and Alcoholism: The Association for the Study of Inebriety, A Case Study." Psy.D. diss. Rutgers University, State University of New Jersey, 1982.

Levine, Harry. "The Discovery of Addiction: Changing Conceptions of Habitual Drunkenness in America." *Journal of Studies on Alcohol* 39, no. 2 (1978): 143–74.

Parish, Joseph. *Alcoholic Inebriety: From a Medical Standpoint.* Philadelphia: P. Blakiston, 1883.

Rush, Benjamin. "Plan for an Asylum for Drunkards to Be Called the Sober House." 1810. Reprinted in *The Autobiography of Benjamin Rush,* ed. G. Corner. Princeton: Princeton University Press, 1948.

Tracy, Sarah "The Foxborough Experiment: Medicalizing Inebriety at the Massachusetts Hospital for Dipsomaniacs and Inebriates." Ph.D. diss., University of Pennsylvania, 1992.

White, William L. *Slaying the Dragon: The History of Addiction Treatment and Recovery in America.* Bloomington, Ill.: Chestnut Health Systems, 1998.

Wilkerson, A. E. "A History of the Concept of Alcoholism as a Disease." D.S.W. diss., University of Pennsylvania, 1966.

Woodward, Samuel. *Essays on Asylums for Inebriates.* Worcester, Mass., 1838. Reprinted in *Nineteenth-Century Medical Attitudes toward Alcoholic Addiction,* ed. Gerald N. Grob. New York: Arno Press, 1981.

Index

Born in New Haven, Connecticut, JOHN W. CROWLEY has lived much of his life in New York State. A graduate of Yale University (B.A., 1967) and of Indiana University (M.A., 1969, Ph.D., 1970), he was on the faculty of Syracuse University for thirty-two years, serving for three of them as English department chair. He is now professor of English at the University of Alabama in Tuscaloosa. Crowley has published numerous books and articles, including a trilogy on the American realist William Dean Howells. His recent work has been primarily in the field of alcohol and addiction studies: *The White Logic: Alcoholism and Gender in American Modernist Fiction* (1994) and *Drunkard's Progress: Narratives of Addiction, Despair, and Recovery* (1999).

WILLIAM L. WHITE is a senior research consultant at Chestnut Health Systems / Lighthouse Institute, where he pursues his interests in addiction-related research, training, and writing. He has a master's degree in addiction studies and more than thirty-five years of experience in the addictions field. White has authored or co-authored more than 120 articles and monographs and eight books. His articles have appeared in such journals as *Addiction, Alcoholism Treatment Quarterly,* and *Contemporary Drug Problems.* His *Slaying the Dragon: The History of Addiction Treatment and Recovery in America* (1998) received the McGovern Family Foundation Award for the best book on addiction recovery. White was also featured in the Bill Moyers's PBS special "Close to Home: Addiction in America" and Showtime's documentary "Smoking, Drinking, and Drugging in the Twentieth Century." He lives with his wife in Port Charlotte, Florida.